SECRET
Tasmania

Philip and Mary Blake

NEW
HOLLAND

First published in Australia in 2002 by
New Holland Publishers (Australia) Pty Ltd
Sydney • Auckland • London • Cape Town

14 Aquatic Drive Frenchs Forest NSW 2086 Australia
218 Lake Road Northcote Auckland New Zealand
86 Edgware Road London W2 2EA United Kingdom
80 McKenzie Street Cape Town 8001 South Africa

4 6 8 10 9 7 5 3

National Library of Australia
Cataloguing-in-Publication Data:

Blake, Philip Gerard, 1949– .
Secret Tasmania.

Bibliography.

Includes index.

ISBN 1 86436 735 0.

1. Tasmania - Description and travel. 2. Tasmania - Social life and customs.
3. Tasmania - History. I. Blake, Mary, 1956- . II. Title.

994.6

Publishing Manager: Anouska Good
Senior Editor: Monica Ban
Designer: Alix Korte
Reproduction: Pica Digital, Singapore
Printer: McPherson's Printing Group, Victoria

This book was typeset in Bembo 11pt

Front cover: Thylacine—a slaughtered Tasmanian; Secret sunset—Tasmanian seascape
Errol Flynn—a famous Tasmanian; Port Arthur—Tasmanian icon.

Contents

Dedication

To my mother, Helen Blake, who always
encouraged me to read and write, and gave
me an Imperial Good Companion
typewriter when I was 14.

Philip

For my family—
the Tasmanian McWhirters.

Mary

Acknowledgments

It's traditional to apologise to one's family for the inconvenience to which they've been subjected during the writing of a book. We're not going to do that. In the last year or two some of the younger members of our family went to see places and things that they were never otherwise likely to visit, and often enjoyed doing so. The times they didn't enjoy were character-building, and they are now a fount of general (though possibly none too useful) knowledge about their State.

We have had the help of a number of specialists, who are acknowledged in the text. We would also like to thank the staff of the Tasmaniana Library (who may only be 'doing their jobs', but do them very well), and Chris Viney, who offered us the chance to write the book.

What's it About?

That's the most common question we've been asked about this book—and it's a good one. The simple answer is that it's about Tasmania's not-so-obvious features—people, places, things and events that aren't known as a part of everyday life. (Some of the things we've included, in fact, *are* part of everyday life, but have a secret or not-so-obvious side. Like the Tasman Bridge, or the Cataract Gorge.)

One of the rewarding things that writing the book has brought us is the input from other people. 'Have you got anything in about the disaster in the gold mine at Cygnet?' was one that led down a blind alley, but opened up another avenue of exploration. 'What about that convict dam in the Midlands that never got finished?' was another. Everybody seems to know something or somebody—but then, this is Tasmania.

When we started to dig for the stories, one thing led to another. The degree of connection between some of the stories was remarkable—especially the historical ones. Tasmania is a small place even today, and there were a lot less people living here in the 19th century, so it's hardly surprising that the same names cropped up again and again in our research. The same Captain Horton, who set up Horton College, was also robbed at his home, 'Somercotes', by Matthew Brady. Sir John Franklin was related to Matthew Flinders and travelled to Australia with him. There is a 'Wingy's Tier' in the Midlands that may or may not be named after Wingy Gunn, and so it goes on.

There are two main parts to a book like this—the research and the writing. Mary, who is a librarian, does the research and I do the writing. We have also dabbled in each other's area, and have made all the important decisions together, so *Secret Tasmania* is very much a joint effort.

We will feel we have succeeded in this book every time a reader looks up from a story and says, 'I didn't know that!'

BASS
STRAIT

TASMANIA

KING
IS
Currie
Grassy

North West Cape

FLINDERS
IS
Whitemark

CAPE BARREN IS

CLARKE IS

HUNTER IS
TREFOIL IS
Cape Grim
Woolnorth
ROBBINS IS
Circular
Head
Rocky
Cape
Smithton
Sisters
Beach
Table Cape
Wynyard
Burnie
Ulverstone
Devonport

Cape
Portland
SWAN IS
WATERHOUSE IS
Low
Head
Port
Dalrymple
George Town
Bellingham
Scottsdale
Herrick
Derby
Pioneer
Moorina
Frome R
Weldborough
St Helens
Gladstone
Eddystone
Point
Ringarooma R
Branxholm

West
Point
Sandy
Cape

Balfour

Mt Sunday

Waratah

Waldheim
Cradle Mtn

Corinna

Zeehan

Queenstown
Strahan

Cape
Sorell
Macquarie
Harbour

THREE
HUMMOCK
IS

Arthur R

Pieman R

White R

Savage R

Ahrberg
Bay

Mt Olympus
St Clair

Darwin
Crater

Mt King
William

L King
William

L St Clair

L Tahune

L Borrington

L Rowallan

Gordon R

Franklin R

Gordon R

L Echo

L Dobson

Twilight
Tarn

L Pedder

Gordon

Mt Mawson

Spreyton
Kindred
Latrobe
Tarleton
Exeter
Frankford
Wilmot
Sheffield
Bridgenorth
Westbury
Mt Roland
Longford
Cressy

Kelso
Beauty Point
Port Sorell

Crescent Bay

Launceston
Cataract Gorge
Illawarra
Perth

Cornwall
Mt Elephant
Fingal

St Marys

Elephant Pass

Upper
Blessington
Blessington
Deddington
Rossarden

Breadalbane

Campbell
Town
Ross

Poatina

Great
Lake

Arthurs L
Steppes
Waddamana

L Sorell

Cornellan
Bay

L Leake

Long Marsh
Dam

Tooms
Lake

L Crescent

Lake

Oatlands
Andover
Bothwell

Nala
Lisdillon
Little
Swanport

Melton
Mowbray

Hamilton

Ouse

Mt Direction

Bicheno

Swansea
Piermont
Mt Mayson
Mt Amos
Freycinet Peninsula

Coles Bay
Oyster
Bay

SCHOUTEN
IS

MARIA
IS

Orford

New Norfolk
Glenorchy
Mt Wellington
Hobart
Kingston

Cornelian
Bay

Sorell
Dunalley

Eaglehawk
Bay
Eaglehawk
Neck
Forestier
Pen
Tasman
Pen
Port Arthur

TASMAN
IS

Huon R

AirWalk
Snug
Woodbridge
Cygnet
Geeveston

NORTH
BRUNY

Storm
Bay

SOUTH
BRUNY
IS

Crescent
Bay

South
West
Cape

South
East
Cape

···· Motorbikes to Zeehan

····· The Franklins' journey

SOUTHERN

OCEAN

TASMAN

SEA

0   100 km

S

Stories from the South

A visit
from
Hell

Anglesea Barracks in Hobart contains
a simple square monument commemorating
the 1967 bushfires—the infamous 'Black
Tuesday' fires that saw Tasmanians forcefully
and tragically reminded of just how
vulnerable the State is to fire.

T he fires on 7 February 1967 were so fearsome
that reports were received (and believed) in
the British Isles of evacuations by sea (and
carried out by submarine, because the surface of the sea was boiling!). The
reality was in some ways even worse—trees snapped off by the force of
firestorm winds, mid-air explosions of flammable gas, huge fireballs racing
through the air, houses gone in minutes, people and animals killed in seconds... For the previous five months, humidity in southern and eastern
Tasmania had been extremely low, and everywhere the grass was long and
dry. January and February have always been the State's most dangerous
months for bushfires, and on 7 February 1967, when there were already
about 80 fires burning, the temperature went up to just under 40°C.
Combined with this were high winds and very low humidity.

Incredibly, some people were still lighting fires—burning off rubbish,
burning off debris on forest floors, or just mischievously lighting fires.

These new fires, and those already burning, joined up like advancing armies and attacked Hobart and the surrounding towns.

Control of these fires in the face of 120-kilometre per hour winds was out of the question. The ferocity of the fires was beyond anything previously encountered in the State.

And the fires were not the only problem. In some places there was water but insufficient pressure. In others, the washers in the water mains were being melted by the heat. On Hobart's Waterworks Road (whose name alone suggested it should be safe), work went ahead on the morning of 7 February to turn off and cut a water main for road construction—a couple of hours after the Hobart fire brigade had called up all its off-duty firefighters. By teatime, some 30 houses in Waterworks Road had been burned down, despite the presence of a large and inaccessible volume of water in the reservoir at the top of the hill.

There were even hoax calls on this day, diverting firefighters from genuine fires. Not that the afternoon of 7 February allowed them to do much—preserving life and property was about as much as they could attempt to do.

Despite heroic efforts, some 1700 farm sheds were burnt, as were 500 vehicles and machines, and about a quarter of a million hectares of farmland and housing. Over 80 000 farm animals died; nearly 1300 houses and over 120 major buildings were destroyed; 7500 people were left homeless; and 62 died. The property cost alone was estimated at $25 million.

As a measure of the seriousness of these fires, in the previous 12 months the highest monthly number of calls to the Hobart Fire Brigade for January 1966 had been 135. On this day, 7 February 1967, there were 130 calls.

These calls were on a service already stretched far beyond its limits. The Hobart Fire Brigade had about 85 staff to draw on, with 10 fire-engines. There was a further auxiliary volunteer force of about 70 at Fern Tree, without fire-engines, and a couple of council firewatch crews with vehicles. The Army too threw its firefighting resources into the fray. That, in essence, was the force lined up in the city to face an enemy whose energy release one expert said 'far exceeded the energy of several atomic explosions.' In the surrounding countryside it was little better. The Tasmanian Forestry Commission was the best-equipped force, with some 70 firefighters ready for action. Their backup was mostly in the form of volunteer rural brigades, variously and often inadequately equipped in every area but courage.

The Risdon Prison, too, played its part, releasing prisoners to fight the fires—and in the case of one prisoner, to help the magistrate who had sent him to prison save his own house! (After the fires, too, the inmates of the prison were to work long and hard, cooking and baking bread for the homeless.)

The aftermath was like a battlefield. Snug, south of Hobart, was virtually destroyed, with 11 people killed. In fact, aerial photographs of the town show an eerie resemblance to Hiroshima, with a few houses still intact in a desert of devastation. Colebrook, Sorell, Taroona, New Norfolk and the western suburbs of Hobart were severely burnt. Survivors of those awful hours described how they spent the time—some face-down in paddocks, some standing in the sea, some hiding under bridges.

It was the first day of the school year, and many children had a startling initiation to school. The children of Sorell School shared the beach and causeway with a circus and its frightened animals. Back at the school, where some of the teachers were fighting spot fires, the temperature in the yard was 63°C. From the Huonville School, children could see their own homes burning down. At Snug, although the school would eventually burn down, it was the safest place for the children to be. At Levendale School the children were to be sent out to the oval until sheets of flame were seen landing on it. They were then evacuated in cars. The Colebrook children lay face down under wet towels in the middle of a ploughed paddock for four hours.

Principals reacted in different ways to the fire—some sent children home, others kept them at school overnight; and in every case they appear to have made the correct decisions for their circumstances. Many were full of praise for the children's coolness (in contrast to the parents described by one principal: '11:25—first parents arrived to claim children and promote panic.') Incredibly, despite several schools burning down, no-one under the age of 23 was killed.

Where did the fires come from? Some were spot fires, caused by burning embers from fires further north. Some were accidentally started by sparks from burning rubbish and the like. But most of them, about 90, were deliberately lit, for the reasons mentioned above.

After this disaster, and the two subsequent reports by D.M. Chambers, Q.C., major changes were made to the structure of firefighting in Tasmania. The *Rural Fires Act 1967* started the process of carrying out the recommendations of the Chambers Report, with its suggestion that at least 200 volunteer rural fire brigades were needed to protect the State against a repetition of 1967's horrors. Under the new order, the State was divided up into Regions and Special Areas, and a command and communications structure was set up that allowed rapid and efficient response as well as pre-emptive action like fire trail cutting and hazard reduction burning. Within just three years, the number of rural fire brigades working under the new Rural Fires Board went from under 50 to five times that many, and their membership was by then over 5000 strong.

The *Fire Service Act 1979* took things a few stages further, establishing the present-day Tasmania Fire Service under the control of the State Fire Commission. Today, all firefighting in the State is under central control. There are still over 240 brigades, including four full-time ones in the four major cities. The remainder are staffed by about 5000 volunteer members, and their firefighting equipment is of a far higher standard of both performance and compatibility than that of 1967. (There is also a lot more of it!) Effective communication was one of the earliest and most serious casualties of the fires, and today's underground telephone cables were installed in an effort to make them less vulnerable to fire and other above-ground catastrophes. The Tasmania Fire Service now has some 800 VHF radios, each with access to 145 channels that allow them not only to communicate with one another but with other Emergency Services, the Forestry Industry and Local Government. Members also carry 2500 personal pagers that allow rapid State-wide response to callouts. The communication network evolved for the fire service is now so effective and has such good coverage that it is used every autumn by the Targa Tasmania international car rally for field communications. (This is one of the reasons why the event runs when it does—at a time when the bush-fire danger is low.) Today, the split between city and rural fire services has been closed up; the well-equipped and highly efficient Tasmania Fire Service we enjoy nowadays (and that some of us take for granted) is a direct descendant of the services that were born out of that day in 1967 when Tasmania had a visit from Hell.

How to get there

The monument at Anglesea Barracks (Davey Street, Hobart) is on a grassed area diagonally opposite the entrance to the Military Museum. It is made of stone from buildings lost in the fires.

'The best little sea boat I ever sailed in'

A walk along the Hobart waterfront is very likely to acquaint you with the brig *Lady Nelson*, either moored or out on the water under sail. Incidentally, if she's out on the water and there is no wind, you may be able to hear the throb of a diesel engine, which tells you that she isn't the original *Lady Nelson*.

T he sail training and charter vessel that sails the Derwent nowadays is a replica of the original, which was lost with all hands in 1825. The engine is just one of the departures from the original design—a safety requirement. One major difference between 'our' vessel and the one that sailed from England in 1800 is that the original, designed by Captain John Schanck R.N., had three sliding keels, each rather like the centreboard in a sailing dinghy, whereas the 20th century model has a fixed keel, deeper hull and 12 tonnes of lead ballast. (The reason for this is that as a working sail training and charter vessel she has to be able to survive an 80% knockdown.) She is also equipped with a wheel in place of the original tiller, radar, electronic navigation aids, watertight bulkheads, fireproof engine room bulkheads and improved crew accommodation. Above the waterline, however, she is almost identical in profile to the original vessel.

The idea of building her came from a suggestion at a 'First-Fleeters' dinner in Sydney that for the Bicentennial celebrations each State should build a replica of a vessel significant to the early history of that State. The *Lady Nelson* was not the original suggestion for Tasmania, but was chosen because she was *the* most significant vessel in the early exploration and settlement of Tasmania. (Both north and south could claim her, so it was hoped—in vain—that divisive parochialism would not interfere with her building.)

The replica was built at Ray Kemp's boatyard at Woodbridge, with a Tasmanian Oak hull, Celery-Top Pine decking and Douglas Fir spars. The total cost was well over half a million dollars, which was raised in fits and starts with a hiatus at the end before final fitting out. Although she was launched in time for her bicentennial target date, she had to take part in the Tall Ships parade under engine power.

Built in Deptford, England, in 1799, Her Majesty's Armed (another difference!) Survey Vessel *Lady Nelson* was 16 metres long, with a beam of 5.5 metres and a carrying capacity of less than 60 tonnes. Her sliding keels gave her a very shallow draught, ideal for the kind of estuarine exploration she was likely to encounter in 'New Holland.'

The original *Lady Nelson* was hardly bristling with artillery—she carried six guns as an 'armed tender', and a single 150-millimetre bore carronade as a supply vessel yet one of her tasks in Australian waters was to guard towns on the coast that had no defence of their own.

Her first voyage, from England to Australia in 1800, was under Lieutenant James Grant. The Dane, Jorgen Jorgenson, attempted en route to hitch a ride to Australia but was turned down by Grant. (Jorgenson's chequered future was to include stints as both second and first mate aboard the ship!)

While she was laid up in Cape Town for repairs to her keels, Grant received a message from Governor King in New South Wales which told him that Bass Strait had been discovered by Bass and Flinders (and that Van Diemen's Land was therefore an island!). He made use of this information on his way to Port Jackson, and the *Lady Nelson* thus became the first vessel to sail through Bass Strait from west to east. Previously, vessels had sailed all the way around the south coast of Tasmania, which was thought to be attached to the mainland.

The *Lady Nelson*'s career, in fact, is a series of firsts:
- Her crew planted the first crops in Victoria.
- She was the first ship in Australia to fly the Union Jack.
- She was the first ship to survey the Hunter River.
- She was the first ship to chart Port Phillip Bay.
- She brought the first settlers to Van Diemen's Land. (In fact, she arrived before Lieutenant Bowen did, and waited for his official arrival.)

- She surveyed the settlement at Port Dalrymple (George Town).
- She brought the first settlers to Sullivans Cove (Hobart).
- She carried the first settlers to Port Dalrymple.
- She brought the first settlers to Newcastle in New South Wales.
- She successfully engaged a French ship in Jervis Bay.
- She carried two lots of passengers from Norfolk Island to Tasmania, where they would eventually settle up the Derwent River at a town they called New Norfolk.

The *Lady Nelson* gave her name to several well-known landmarks in Tasmania and further afield. Mount Nelson is named after her, as is Lady Nelson Creek between George Town and Launceston. Less obvious is Tinderbox. The *Lady Nelson* was so small that when she joined her first convoy to come out from England, the sailors in bigger ships called her 'HMS Tinderbox,' and the nickname stuck—both to the ship and to the place.

Wrecked at Port Macquarie in 1821, she was repaired and restored for the final chapter of her life, as a supply vessel on the eastern and northern coasts of Australia. It was on one of these supply trips, looking for buffalo to supply meat to Fort Dundas on Bathurst Island, that she would end her days in bizarre circumstances. In 1825 she sailed across the Banda Sea to call at the island of Babar, an island inhabited by native pirates. While trading with the natives, the crew made the mistake of calling out abuse to a woman as she relieved herself on the beach. She called on her menfolk to kill them all, which they did. The *Lady Nelson* was then run aground and burned. (Another ship, the *Stedcombe*, which went to look for her, suffered the same fate—most of her crew being beheaded.) A carronade, presumably from the *Lady Nelson*, is still on the island.

It is somehow fitting that man, and not the sea, was responsible for the end of what Governor Lachlan Macquarie called 'the best little sea boat I ever sailed in.' It is still possible to see whether you agree with the Governor. On Saturdays, when not under charter, the *Lady Nelson* runs 1½-hour trips on the Derwent at very low prices—only $5 per person at the time of writing.

How to get there

There aren't that many square-rigged sailing ships in the Hobart docks. *Lady Nelson* is the white one, usually moored beside Elizabeth Pier.

In like
Flynn

'...you knew where you stood with Errol:
he would always let you down.'

David Niven's comment about one of Tasmania's most famous sons tells us much of what we need to know about Errol Flynn, the man. Flynn the film star played swashbuckling roles in about 50 films (most notably *Captain Blood* and *Robin Hood*), and made (and lost) millions of dollars. If we can believe the possibly embellished stories of his autobiography, *My Wicked, Wicked Ways*, Flynn also led a spectacular life even before he hit the silver screen—as a gold miner, white slaver, soldier of fortune and hero of the phrase, 'In like Flynn'.

Flynn the schoolboy roamed the streets of suburban Hobart, living in a succession of houses from the humble to the manorial. He was born in Hobart in 1909, to a teenage mother and an older, academic father. His first home here was the boarding house 'Mildura', at 52 Warwick Street. As his father's career as a lecturer in marine botany and biology blossomed, their accommodation moved up the social scale.

From 1914 to 1916, the five- and six-year-old Errol played in the gardens of 'Glen Garie', 10 Darcy Street, South Hobart. The next two years were spent in more prosperous accommodation not far away, as Professor Flynn and his family lived in one of the most desirable parts of Hobart at what is now 'Ardglen', 296 Davey Street (then called Holebrook Place). Their next address was 60 Duke Street, Sandy Bay. (The house now has a plate identifying it as 'Flynn's Cottage'.)

His family moved to Sydney, and then London in the early 1920s, but Professor Flynn's academic career brought him and Errol back to Hobart in 1924. Father and son lived at 12 Aberdeen Street, Glebe, in a very attractive Victorian Italianate house overlooking the parklands of the Queen's Domain and the magnificent harbour.

Errol was by now 15, and beginning to show the character that would 'endear' him in later years to people like David Niven. The shed at 12 Aberdeen Street still bears the scars of his attempt to burn it down—and his career at Hobart High School was to last only one year. His expulsion was the result of the school authorities' shortsighted view of a ballistic experiment with ice-cream cones on a group of dignitaries which included the school principal. (The school building, in Letitia Street, is now Turnbull Family Funerals—a career change of which Flynn would surely approve.)

His early life was a succession of lurches from one anti-authoritarian prank to another—a curious way of life for someone brought up in a conservative town like Hobart. For example, when asked (at an early age) to get down off the rigging of a ship in Hobart harbour, he complied—and then threw all the ship's buckets over the side. One notorious childhood exploit (which he described as an 'experiment') was feeding a piece of fatty pork on a long string to one of the family ducks; the duck was keen enough to eat it, but its digestive system was equally keen to get rid of it. The whole process, 'from beak to rectum', says Flynn, took about two minutes. Holding the string in one hand, he then fed the pork to another duck, and another... His father beat him with an umbrella for that one, and was not impressed by Errol's remarks about his own experiments with living creatures.

This rebellious streak could be put down to a very unsettled childhood with parents who showed little interest in him, or to a lengthy period as the only child, or to innate wickedness, perhaps...

And yet his personality was magnetic. One school friend describes walking down the street with the young Flynn as positively embarrassing, because of the attention he drew from women. This sheer physical attractiveness, coupled with an obvious natural intelligence, would eventually make him his fortune as a movie actor; while his early life surrounded by all things nautical would start a lifelong affair with the only thing, perhaps, Errol Flynn ever really loved—the sea.

Friends
Park

The Friends Park in Mellifont
Street, West Hobart, is an unusual site
for a children's playground, in that it
contains about 60 gravestones.

There are no human remains under your feet; they were removed in 1936. The reason for the gravestones is that this 0.2-hectare piece of parkland was once the Friends' burial ground. It was sold for five shillings to the Society of Friends as a cemetery by William Shoobridge, who has been described as 'a Wesleyan with Quaker leanings.' He died soon after, and became one of its first tenants.

Another headstone is that of George Washington Walker, founder of the Hobart Savings Bank. The gravestones are very simple—a reflection of the Quaker way and their rejection of the pomp of organised religion.

The 8-metre wooden sculpture is a recent addition. A cypress tree planted in the 1860s, and long since dead, used to adorn the park, its four main branches lopped off for safety. The stumps of the branches have been chainsawed and polished by local sculptor Roland Gabatel into four huge figures, two male and two female, each holding a bird.

The park is a pleasant place to spend half an hour, and both the gravestones and the sculpture provide something to reflect on while you plan the rest of your safari into *Secret Tasmania*.

Keen as...

If you look in the general direction of
Mount Wellington from a number of Hobart's
busier streets, you will see a sign reading 'Keens
Curry' written in white stones on the
hillside above South Hobart.

This is a sign with a long history, and it is now on the Tasmanian Heritage Register. At the time of its construction, however, its owner was removed from quite a number of Christmas card lists.

When Joseph Keen arrived in Hobart from England in the late 1840s, he brought with him a formula for curry powder, and proceeded to make and market it from a factory in Kingston (an ideal location, given Tasmanians' known and continuing fondness for curried scallops). The curry powder was so successful that it won a special plaque at the Intercolonial Exhibition of 1866.

When Joseph was dying (and not a moment before) he passed on the formula to his wife Annie—daughter of George Burrows, of the mutiny on the *Bounty*. (He also passed on 24 children, which suggests that indulgence in the product did him no harm!) Annie continued to manufacture the product until she too was ready to pass on, at which stage the secret formula was given to her son-in-law Horace Watson.

Watson was the man who in 1905 or thereabouts bought the land above Stoney Steps Road, on what is now known as Keens Curry Hill, and did the hard work of arranging and painting the stones to make the 20-metre high sign.

Out of the Blue: A History of Reckitt and Colman in Australia mentions that there was an outcry in Hobart about the disfigurement of the city, quelled by Horace pointing out that he had a right to put up whatever sign he liked on his own land. What the book does not mention is that there was already a sign on the site—and one which would have curried rather more favour with the locals. It read 'VR 60', and had been erected 10 years before to commemorate the 60th year of the reign of Queen Victoria. Watson's son Ted was ordered to paint out the sign for security reasons during World War II. One wonders what these security reasons were, since the sign was only visible by day—as indeed were a lot of other equally obvious landmarks and targets.

When Horace sold the company (including the land and the sign on it) to A.C. Ferrall of Launceston in 1951, one condition of the sale was that the recipe for the curry powder would continue to be kept secret. Ferrall's were enthusiastic about selling Keen's Traditional Curry Powder on the mainland, but it was pointed out to them by another of their large customers, Reckitt and Colman, that this might cause a trademark battle with their own Keen's Mustard (incredibly, no relation). Ferrall's therefore decided to sell to Reckitt and Colman. Alec Thompson, Works Director of Reckitt and Colman, now acquired the secret, and its manufacture moved to Redfern in Sydney. (If you find it difficult to believe that Keen's Mustard and Keen's Curry started out as two separate companies, study the small logos on their containers. Keen's Curry has a scallop shell, while Keen's Mustard has a bull's head.)

One morning in 1926, Hobartians looking up at the sign were horrified to see that it now read 'Hell's curse.' University students were blamed for this piece of Commemoration Day mischief. The company, never slow to pass up on a publicity opportunity, said that it should have read 'Heav'n's bless'n.' And sure enough, that's what it read the following year…

In 1962 the students were back at it, turning it into 'Fred's Folly' (from the title of the University Revue that year); and more recently when there was a dispute about the projected Mount Wellington cable car project, it was altered to read 'No cable car.'

Keen's Curry is now the leading brand of curry powder in Australia; and a sign that was once vilified as a blot on the landscape has now become a part of the fabric of Hobart—as well as a reminder that Tasmania was the birthplace of all those lovely curries.

Cornelian Bay and the boatsheds

If you mention Cornelian Bay to
anyone from Hobart, they'll immediately
assume you're talking about the cemetery.
But there is a lot more to this quiet bay
than the cemetery on its outer point.

Before European settlement, Cornelian Bay was occupied by the Oyster Bay and Southeast groups of the Tasmanian Aboriginal people, and traces of their occupation can still be found (and left where they are!) in the middens and shell scatters between Pipe Clay Point and the Botanic Gardens. Pipe Clay Point is the point at the end of the line of boathouses on the southern side of the bay, on the opposite arm of the bay from the cemetery.

Although today it is surrounded by streets of suburban houses and sports grounds, in its early history 'this quiet bay' was anything but quiet. It housed a red light district, it was a place to careen whaling ships, it had a gypsy camp—and it had its own horse racecourse! It was a popular bathing spot, too, and it wasn't quiet even in the water, as three boys found in 1850:

Voracity of the Shark
Last week while three of Mr Hull's sons were bathing in the sandy bay at New Town, called Cornelian Bay, one of the boys observed

the dorsal fin of a shark above the water a few yards from him; he immediately called to his companions, and they hurried out of the water. He himself was followed by the shark with such rapidity that as he ran up on the beach, the shark, by the rapidity of his motion, became shoaled on the sand. The boys seeing its predicament, immediately seized the monster, dragged it by main force out of the water, and killed it with a large stone. It measured five feet ten inches in length and there is very little doubt of its sanguinary intentions. This is not the only instance of the dangerous nature of the sharks in Cornelian Bay; as a gentleman, recently, while wiping his feet on the bank, after bathing, saw a shark come up to the shore in front of him, and look up, as if with a longing desire to make a breakfast upon him. (*Hobart Town Advertiser*)

Today there is a restaurant, 'The Cornelian Bay Boat House', on the foreshore, with a splendid view of the Tasman Bridge and, closer by, the boatsheds. These boatsheds, about 30 of them, were built early in the 20th century on poles sunk at the water's edge, and have been in continuous use ever since. During the Depression, in fact, they were permanently occupied.

While it is reasonable to suppose that anyone owning a boatshed is interested in boats and the sea, few of the boatsheds are used for storing boats. They are used as urban 'shacks' by their owners, who visit them for barbecues, parties, overnight stays, or just to sit and enjoy the atmosphere. All have running water, and most appear to have electricity.

Their general appearance ranges from down-at-heel to architect-renovated, from flaky (literally) to shipshape, and from determinedly raffish to quietly conservative. They have names ('Capri', 'Rothsay') and numbers and permits for being structures built on Crown land. Some have little gardens clutching at the slopes above them, and all have spectacular views.

A curious trend in the owners is that most of them are male, none are under 30 years of age and most of them have university qualifications!

How to get there

You can see the boatsheds *en masse* from anywhere along the shore by the restaurant, and you can get a closer look at them by taking the Cornelian Bay Walking Track, which runs parallel to the bikeway and goes from Cornelian Bay back to the Domain. One of the best features of this easy walk is that it has a restaurant at either end.

Jewish Receiving House and Cemetery

While you're visiting Cornelian
Bay, it's worth having a look at the
Jewish Receiving House and Cemetery
on Queen's Walk (the road behind The
Cornelian Bay Boat House restaurant).

T he Receiving House is on the Tasmanian Heritage
Register, where it is described as 'a tiny weather-
board building with gabled roof and trapezoidal
windows and a pair of panelled central front doors.' Its architecture is
described as 'Victorian Egyptian'—not the nationality one would
expect! Incidentally, if you're curious about the choice of such a prime
piece of real estate for the Cornelian Bay cemetery, the reason for it is
quite simple—it was on a peninsula, so it was never likely to be
surrounded by houses, and was therefore equally unlikely to become a
disease hazard, as many early cemeteries were. Drainage and general
standards of hygiene were not the same in the 19th century as they are
today. Nor was a human cadaver viewed then as such a biological
hazard as it is today.

If you go up on the hill today...

...you're sure of a big surprise...
as long as it's before dawn on the
first day of May, that is.

As the sun rises over the Tasman Peninsula and picks out the highest thing it can reach—the top of Mount Wellington—it also illuminates half a dozen bizarrely-dressed people, wearing bells on their legs and flowers on their hats. And they're dancing.

On top of Mount Wellington in the pre-dawn hours of 1 May, it is not warm. The average overnight temperature at this time of year is 8°C, but Mount Wellington is over 1270 metres above sea level, and it's about 8°C less up there.

The people in white are Morris Dancers. They're a Morris dancing 'side' called the Jolley Hatters, and the form of dance they are doing is so old that no-one is absolutely sure where it comes from. (Sir Thomas Beecham is reputed to have said that people should be prepared to try anything once—with the exception of incest and Morris dancing.)

Morris dancing is certainly a traditional English dance form, but 'Morris' may be a corruption of 'Moorish', or it could even come from the Spanish or French 'Moresque.' Another explanation of the dance style's origins places it in pre-Christian times, as a fertility dance or war dance.

In May, in the Northern Hemisphere, it's a fertility dance. In fact it's often danced in association with that great phallic symbol, the maypole. In Tasmania it's autumn, which is a strange time for fertility dancing—especially with the temperature hovering around the zero mark.

You'll find both men and women dancing here, which is somewhat of a departure from the early tradition. As late as the 19th century, English Morris sides were exclusively male, and often limited to members of one particular family in a village. Individual villages had their own style of dancing, too, which was known as the 'tradition'. Some Morris sides specialise in individual traditions—the Jolley Hatters adhere to several traditions. (The 'Jolley Hatters' name, incidentally, comes from a Hobart inn and brewery of the last century.)

The dancers sometimes carry sticks in their hands, in figures very reminiscent of fencing (with swords, not pickets), while at other times the dances involve elaborate movements with waved handkerchiefs, which may symbolise bunches of flowers. You may notice, too, a strange figure in a smock, capering about in the middle of the dance, yelling jokes and comments for your benefit and correcting people who make mistakes. This is The Fool, another very old traditional English figure. The Fool's job in Morris dancing is to bridge the gap between performer and spectator, preferably in an entertaining way!

So why do Morris dancers do it? Nowadays it's simply for the love of dancing and English folk tradition. And one of the traditions is that you dance before dawn on Mayday…There is at least one other Morris dancing side in Tasmania—the Longford Morris—and a good many of them turn up on top of Mount Wellington, and stay with the Jolley Hatters as they dance in various other spots around Hobart. (Incidentally, if you do decide to drive up Mount Wellington to see the Morris dancers and enjoy the spectacular view of Hobart, do it carefully. The Pinnacle Road is narrow and twisty, and may well be icy. But there will be tracks to follow—the dancers'!)

How to get there

You really want to do this? Okay, first get out of bed at 5.30 a.m. Davey Street out of Hobart becomes the Huon Road (B64). Follow this until you reach the Pinnacle Road (C616) on your right at Fern Tree. Now follow that to the top of Mount Wellington. You will be made welcome.

Tasman
Bridge

One of Hobart's real landmarks
is the graceful arch of the Tasman Bridge.
And yet, if you study it closely, you can see
that it's not as symmetrical, or quite
as graceful, as it might be.

T he spans of the Tasman Bridge stride regularly across the river from Hobart's Western Shore, but just before they get to the Eastern Shore there is one wider gap. This gap marks the location of an engineering *tour de force* where the bridge was repaired after the Tasman Bridge Disaster of 1975. It also marks the spot where a 10 000-tonne ship lies in the deep silt at the bottom of the Derwent.

On the night of 5 January, just before 9.30 p.m., the bridge was hit by the 10 500-tonne bulk ore carrier *Lake Illawarra*, which had strayed off course and missed the main navigation piers of the bridge (which are massively reinforced in case they are brushed by a ship). The collision took out two of the piers and the three spans they supported, and a piece of the roadway as long as a football pitch fell on the ship, sinking it under 7000 tonnes of concrete in 30 metres of water. Seven crew members died, and five other people were killed when their cars plunged off the bridge into the river. Newspaper photographs of the time show two cars literally hanging over the edge of the bridge. One of these had actually slid over the edge while stopping. The other had stopped in time on the roadway, but was hit from behind by another car and pushed over the brink. The occupants of the two cars did their best to wave down other cars to prevent anyone else driving over the edge. (It was cruel luck that one of the drivers waving down the traffic had already lost an arm in a railway accident many years before.)

The city almost stopped overnight. At that time the only way for the Eastern Shore's 50 000 residents to get to Hobart apart from the Tasman Bridge was the 52-kilometre trip through Bridgewater.

By the very next day, a ferry fleet was up and running. The *Cartela* joined the *Matthew Brady* and the *James McCabe*, which were already operating a service for Robert Clifford's Sullivans Cove Ferry Company; these three were soon joined by the Bruny Island ferry *Mangana*. Soon to follow were the *Martin Cash*, the *Lawrence Kavanagh* and the *Michael Howe*—a hovercraft. Here, in fact, was where Robert Clifford started his Incat boatbuilding empire. His 'bushranger' ferry fleet paved the way for the *Jeremiah Ryan*, first of the fast catamarans that were to become known all over the world. The 18.5-metre *Jeremiah Ryan* carried 150 passengers at 25 knots. When he realised the potential of these catamaran ferries, Clifford stated publicly that he could see himself becoming a boatbuilder rather than a ferry operator, and that the sales of the boats could be worth up to $2 million a year for Tasmania. (They were soon worth at least 50 times that.)

The problem of emergency services for the Eastern Shore was solved by two fast army landing barges which were placed at their disposal. (Several babies were born in the middle of the Derwent as a result.)

The collapse of the bridge immediately highlighted the need for better access between Eastern and Western shores, and within a week the Australian Army's top bridge expert was looking at sites for an alternative Bailey bridge or floating bridge further up the river. Also within a week the reconstruction of the 'goat-track' Old Beach Road began. This was finished in record time and has since been a real asset to the Eastern Shore.

Within two months of the disaster the American bridge expert A.M. Voorhees was commissioned to carry out a study for a second permanent bridge across the Derwent. By December 1975 the longest Bailey bridge ever built in Australia was in place at Dowsings Point; meanwhile the twin tasks of assessing the damage and planning the repairs to the Tasman Bridge were under way.

Sir Allan Knight, former Hydro-Electric Commissioner, was involved with the Tasman Bridge disaster in many ways—first as the designer of the original floating bridge across the Derwent, then (after the fall of the Tasman Bridge) as the builder of the Kangaroo Bay ferry terminal and Chairman of the Tasman Bridge Restoration Commission, and finally as the original designer of the composite beam construction system used for the final roadway repair span. (The world prototype of this form of bridge construction is to be found on Proctor's Road between Kingston and Hobart, where it was built in the 1930s.)

The contract to repair the bridge was given to John Holland (Constructions), and the tricky job began. At first there was talk of salvaging the *Lake Illawarra*, but this was abandoned, so the piers could not be replaced in their original positions. One new pier (pier 19) was built in the gap, offset from the centre. The surviving end piers, 17 and 20, were demolished and replaced (while the roadway was still supported!). Pier 18 was never replaced, and still lies at the bottom of the river. The method used was that six new pre-stressed concrete beams (the same method used in the original construction) would span the small gap (42.5 metres), while four high-tensile steel box girders were to go across the larger gap. These were 85 metres long, and weighed over 200 tonnes each. All of these were built upriver at Wilkinson's Point, and came down the river (gently) on barges; the gap was finally closed when the first girder was lifted into position just over two years after the disaster.

The reconstruction of the Tasman Bridge was completed two months ahead of schedule, despite a number of strikes and minor industrial disputes during the work, and it was finally opened on 8 October 1977.

If you drive across the Tasman Bridge today, you will notice that it has five lanes compared to the original four—a modification incorporated into the repair work by dispensing with the existing footpath and hanging a new one out over the water. You may also notice that the traffic stops occasionally; this happens whenever a large ship passes under the bridge.

Further up the river is perhaps the most lasting reminder of the disaster—the Bowen Bridge, the permanent replacement for the Dowsings Point Bailey bridge.

The final word should be left to Sir Allan Knight, veteran of many a tricky engineering problem in his days as Hydro-Electric Commissioner: 'I doubt whether a more difficult engineering job has been carried to a successful conclusion anywhere.'

How to get there

You really can't miss the Tasman Bridge. If you want to see what's under the water, the Tasmanian Museum and Art Gallery has a scale model of the whole scene in its Small Shipping Room, showing the bridge, the river surface and the *Lake Illawarra* lying on the river bed.

The corpse in the fountain

A whole generation is growing up that
has no idea why their elders call the roundabout at the end of the Brooker Highway
'the Railway Roundabout.'

T he answer is, of course, that there used to be a railway
station very close to the roundabout. It has now been
remodelled into the ABC building. Very few people
get to see the centre of the roundabout—they are usually too busy driving
around it—but it does deserve a closer look.

The fountain in the centre was built by the people of Hobart as a monument to the 47 Mayors and Lord Mayors of the city since 1853, and its
design was decided by a competition.

The centre has three entrances in the form of subways under the road;
you can walk through these and admire the fountain and the little gardens,
which you can't see at all clearly from road level without being run over.
It has three tiers of gardens, with the two-tiered fountain at their centre,
and it contains 10 plaques with the names of all the Mayors and Lord
Mayors engraved on them. The Honey Locust trees around the perimeter,
a grafted variety of Gleditsia called 'Sunburst', are glorious in spring.

One of the criteria for the design was that it had to be built for £7000 or less. The Assessor, in awarding the prize for the winning design (from 19 entries), said he thought it would cost a further £600. (Its eventual cost was £12,000.)

The fountain was in the news at the end of the 20th century. One reason was that it had been allowed to fall into disrepair, and was no longer the experience in water and light that its three designers (Messrs. Cuthbert, Parr and Cooper) intended it to be. In fact Roderick Cuthbert, designer of the fountain's hydraulic system, wrote to *The Mercury* in 1997 to say that he was 'horrified and disappointed' at its condition. Thirty-four years before, he and his associates had designed the fountain with a sequencing system that changed the water patterns every 10 minutes, with some patterns completely enclosing the 12-metre spire, others bouncing off it, and the whole thing being lit by day through light ports and by night through fluorescent tubes. 'Now', wrote Cuthbert, 'the pattern is reduced to a fixed, meaningless mass of badly adjusted jets, some of them blocked due to lack of maintenance.' (It has since been repaired.)

Another event that pushed the fountain into the news was the discovery in November 1999 of the naked, burnt body of a man in the lower pool. The unfortunate man was William George Fisher, late of Dunalley but then homeless. An inquest found that he had died of drowning, possibly while attempting to relieve the pain of third-degree burns he had suffered about half a kilometre away on the Domain, where his burnt clothes were found. How exactly he met his lonely death will probably never be known unless someone comes forward with more information.

Despite its recently controversial history, the fountain roundabout is well worth a visit. It is an unusual and remarkably peaceful centrepiece to one of Hobart's busiest traffic junctions.

How to get there

The roundabout is hard to miss; but in case you're not a local, it's the big roundabout at the end of the Brooker Highway, where it meets Liverpool Street.

April
Fool's
Day revisited

Many of us would see it as an
amusing irony that the first parking meter
in Tasmania (in fact, the first parking meter
in Australia) was launched, fired up,
and fed on 1 April 1955.

When he stepped up on April Fools' Day to put the first
meter into operation, the then Lord Mayor, Mr Park,
described it as the first step by the Hobart City
Council to get back control of its own streets. (It would be interesting to
compare the meaning of the same words if they were said today.)

The first meter was a Venner 'Park-O-Meter', made in England. It was
in Collins Street, Hobart, and was handily placed outside the Commercial
Bank of Australia for depositing its loads of threepenny and sixpenny coins.
For sixpence (5 cents), a motorist could park for half an hour, and then had
to move on.

The Lord Mayor made a commitment that the profits from parking fees and fines (incurred by overstaying one's 'right of sojourn') would be used entirely for providing off-street parking.

Two hundred Park-O-Meters were installed at first, but were soon followed by 330 more. The meters were expected to pay for themselves in about 13 months, and they did. That they began to do so right away was illustrated in *The Mercury* four days later with a picture of an anguished driver running towards his car, where a gloating meter attendant held out his parking ticket.

In the Lord Mayor's report for that year, he reported that 'Whilst there are still some fines for over-parking, it is hoped that, in time, there will be none, indicating that the meters are being used properly and motorists are making the optimum use of the space available.' He goes on to say 'some vandalism and mischievous pranks have occurred sporadically...'

The meters survived, however, and the promise to make them pay for off-street parking was kept. In 1968, just 13 years later, the multi-storey car park in Argyle Street opened; it was paid for entirely by the Park-O-Meters and by the fines that the Lord Mayor hoped would gradually peter out.

Walking
Sullivans
Cove

You could start a walk around
Sullivans Cove, Hobart's harbour area,
from almost anywhere, but we suggest
you drive along Castray Esplanade past
Salamanca Place until you see a little park
above you on the right, with what
looks like a sailing ship's white mast
sticking up out of the lawn.

T his little oasis is Princes Park. Set as it is on some
fairly valuable real estate, it affirms the lifestyle
values that were publicly and visibly forgotten by the
builders of the hideous Empress Towers next door. Before you go into the
park, take a look at the tiny octagonal 'gazebo' on the bottom right-hand
corner. This is the Tide House, from which all Tasmania's tidal
distances are measured.

The 'ship's mast' is part of the old semaphore system used to alert the
good folk of Hobart to news. This included ship arrivals, and other items
like convicts escaping from Port Arthur.

If you walk up through Princes Park to Runnymede Street, and turn left,
you'll see Arthur Circus, a perfect circle of workmen's cottages which could
still be in the 19th century if they had horses instead of horsepower parked
in their driveways. Take a wander around this charming circle, which must

contain some of Australia's smallest detached houses—some of which are only just detached. Attempts to swing a cat between them would cause injury to the swinger, let alone the cat.

Go back down Runnymede Street, then, towards the swish Lenna Hotel on your right, which was originally the mansion of shipping magnate Alexander McGregor. Just before you reach Lenna, turn left into McGregor Street and stroll along to the Battery Point Guest House. The downstairs guestroom has been transformed into a stateroom from the *Titanic*, complete with replica Union Star Line furniture and real fish swimming past the portholes!

Continue along McGregor Street until you reach the T-junction with Kelly Street. Here you turn right and head for Kelly's Steps. Before you go down the steps, however, there are some points of interest at the top. No. 1 Kelly Street is the Kelly Street Writers' Cottage, maintained for visiting writers and artists by the Salamanca Arts Centre. Opposite is a car park, at the end of which you will see a free-standing door, without a wall around it. This puzzling structure leads into the Battery Point Garden Studio.

While you're in the car park, take a look through the window of the low building to which it belongs. This was once known as the Howroyd and Forward building, after the firm of architects who designed it (and first used it). It hangs like a great claw on the side of a cliff, and much of the cliff remains inside it. As you go down Kelly's Steps, this building 'follows' you on your right, so you can get a good look at a remarkable piece of architecture. The steps themselves were built by the 19th century whaling captain, James Kelly.

The alleyway at the bottom takes you out past the Peacock Theatre and a number of small shops to Salamanca Place, Hobart's artiest thoroughfare. The whole Salamanca Place area has been turned into a labyrinthine colony of galleries, shops, entertainments and luxury accommodation units. Spend some time here if you like, although it's worth a separate visit, or wander on towards the Tasman Fountain on its hillock of greenery in front of Parliament House. Built to commemorate the landing of Dutch explorer Abel Tasman in 1642, it features models of his ships, the *Heemskirk* and the *Zeehan*.

If you now (carefully) cross the streets between the fountain and the waterfront, you'll see a restaurant complex with a marina behind it. If you stroll along the piers of this marina you'll almost certainly get a good look at a variety of boats. In fact, one of the best things about the Hobart docks is that you never know what you'll see. (We've seen a fairy penguin swimming quite unconcernedly under the piers.)

On your right, you may see the distinctive orange finish of the *Aurora Australis*, the Antarctic supply vessel (unless she's away supplying our Antarctic expeditioners). Or you could spot one of the Incat catamarans, moored during sea trials or setting off on a delivery voyage. Walking on around the waterfront, you may see the replica of the brig *Norfolk*, and the original *May Queen*, the last of Tasmania's great fleet of trading ketches. You will then find yourself on Brooke Street Pier, where a gaggle of ferries waits to take visitors for a cruise on the river. It was from Brooke Street Pier that the hop-pickers used to set sail for the Derwent Valley at the start of the season; this departure was a minor festival in its own right.

While the *May Queen* has been the victim of near-terminal dithering about its fate, the Hobart Marine Board were able to behave very decisively when it came to relocating themselves. Originally they were based in the two-storey building that looks out over the ferries (and their tide gauge can still be seen on the front of it); but this building is today literally over-shadowed by the vast brown thing they built across the street.

In fact, it's almost worth hurrying along this part of the walk, to get past the bottom end of Elizabeth Street and three of Hobart's great mono-liths—the one just mentioned and two others that were built by the then Hydro-Electric Commission. But we do still need to pause here for a second and reflect that we're standing in the footsteps of one of history's great explorers. In 1912, Roald Amundsen walked up this street to the GPO (whose clock tower you can see a couple of blocks up on the right) to send a telegram to the King of Norway saying that he had reached the South Pole. (If the wind's blowing from the South, you may be uncom-fortably reminded that Antarctica is the next land mass in that direction!)

Elizabeth Pier is the next pier along, and what was once just a shed has now been turned into accommodation apartments, reception centres and restaurants, all surrounded by the doings of the harbour. These doings include Tasmania's own sail training vessel, the *Lady Nelson*. This replica of one of Australia's most important early vessels is often tied up beside Elizabeth Pier.

Take a left into Argyle Street and you're in Mawson Place, which is named after Australia's own Antarctic adventurer. Mawson Place occupies one side of Constitution Dock, the final mooring of most of the fleet in the Sydney–Hobart yacht race. (Of late, the lead yachts have been too huge to fit through the entrance.)

If you look up Argyle Street, you'll see the Carnegie Library on the corner of Davey and Argyle streets. This building was built with a £7000 grant from the Scottish-American philanthropist Andrew Carnegie—a grant which was almost lost to the city as a result of dithering and dishonesty by the City Fathers. Carnegie's grant for the new State Library was made on several conditions—a suitable site had to be provided, annual running expenses guaranteed, a free lending department established and a perpetual lease at a nominal rent guaranteed. The Council maundered over the site, they even attempted not to fulfil the 'peppercorn rent' condition; but they rapidly backtracked when the Chairman of the Library Trustees resigned and wrote to Andrew Carnegie telling him what they were up to. If you have time to look inside this building, home of Hobart's first public library, you'll see what splendour we nearly missed out on.

Just a little further along Davey Street you can see the last remaining piece of the original water frontage. At the left of the old Customs House, it looks like someone's very steep backyard, but it's where the land stopped in the days before the present wharf area was reclaimed from the sea.

As you walk on along the Davey Street side of Constitution Dock, you can see the old and the new and something in between. On your left is the Grand Chancellor Hotel; on the right, in Hunter Street, the warehouses that once housed the enormous IXL jam factory; and in between, the gasometer-styled concert hall which is now the home of the Tasmanian Symphony Orchestra.

Hunter Street itself is named after Hunter Island, previously separate from the mainland and approached by a causeway. The path of this causeway is marked by small bronze plaques on the ground, as is the outline of the old Hunter Island itself. Just past the bridge and memorial at the end of Victoria Dock (the one with the fishing fleet), you will see that one warehouse complex now houses the University of Tasmania Centre for the Arts.

You've now come more or less to the end of this walk, and if you've left a car on Castray Esplanade it's time to head back and get it. Take a slightly different route by walking around the opposite sides of the docks, perhaps. If you cross the Victoria Dock Bridge (more Hunter Island plaques on the ground here) you'll see on the rocks the Stephen Walker sculpture *Heading South*, which depicts seals and sea birds. Real birds enjoy perching on these, and unless they've been recently cleaned, you'll notice that they are coated with what used to be an important trading commodity in Tasmania. Several hundred tons of guano a year used to be scavenged by Tasmanian whalers and sold to growers all over the world as fertiliser.

Our seagulls are still doing their best…

Tunnel
Hill

Driving over Tunnel Hill, on
the way from Hobart to the airport,
how many of us have ever wondered
how it got its name?

N aturally it was because of a tunnel—the tunnel that allowed the Sorell railway line to pass steeply through the hillside at that point. Built in 1891, the tunnel echoed to the thunder of trains until 1926, when the line was closed after running at a loss for the previous 34 years! During World War II, the tunnel was used by the Defence Department to store the records from Anglesea Barracks.

In 1972, 65 metres of the tunnel and a couple of hectares of land were sold for $3000 to Mr Janos Pasztor. He planned to clear out the silted-up entrance and establish a canopied picnic/barbecue area in it. (His reason for buying it, he said, was that it reminded him of his native Transylvania.) By 1978 he had renovated the tunnel, clearing out 1.5 metres of silt from the entrance and closing it off with a roller door. He then put the tunnel up for sale, with an asking price of $50,000. It did not sell.

The other end of the tunnel has been used since 1957 by the Physics Department of the University of Tasmania and the Australian Antarctic Division for cosmic ray research. The instruments here are an important part of a worldwide network that covers every continent except Africa.

Cosmic rays (streams of protons, probably from exploding stars) hit the earth all the time at the speed of light. In doing so, they shatter atoms in the atmosphere, causing them to radiate particles. Some of these particles, called muons, hit the ground with enough energy to penetrate deep (over 2 kilometres!) underground. The tunnel is ideal for studying these particles, as it provides a 'filter' of rock overhead to screen out the non-penetrating muons. Those that do penetrate can therefore be deduced to have resulted from impacts of more than a certain size, which tells researchers about the amount of energy in the cosmic rays. Readings from the instruments in the tunnel can then be compared with those on the surface at the university, which receive the input from space unencumbered.

At Mawson Base in Antarctica there are another two sets of instruments, on the surface and 11 metres underground. The sites in Tasmania and Antarctica provide data for the cosmic ray bombardment of the whole Southern Hemisphere, up to the equator. This is a field in which Tasmanian scientists have led the world for 50 years.

The study of cosmic rays helps in determining the origin of the universe and in the study of our own solar system and galaxy (both of whose magnetic fields create small but identifiable variations in the trajectory of cosmic rays).

And it happens beside the road on the way from Hobart to the airport!

How to get there

The tunnel is marked on the *Tasmanian Towns Street Atlas*. Take Cambridge Road (C329) for Sorell. At the top of the hill is a turnoff for Mount Rumney (C328) and Old Coach Road. Park anywhere here; you are on top of the tunnel. Down Cambridge Road is the University half, and down Old Coach Road is the privately owned half.

Thanks to Dr Marc Duldig, Australian Antarctic Division, for explaining cosmic rays in words of one syllable.

From
drudgery
to fudgery

The staff at the Island Produce
Fudge Factory look happy. Maybe it's
because of the unlimited goodies available
to them—a kind of constant temper-
sweetener. It's certainly nothing to do
with the history of the site where they
work, which, if you believe in ghosts,
would be among the most haunted
places in Tasmania.

T he factory stands in Degraves Street, North Hobart, on part of the site of what was once 'The Female Factory.' This euphemistic title was given to it at its opening in 1828, presumably to cover up the fact that it was actually a women's prison. It was built on the site of an old distillery, to replace the four rooms in the Hobart Town Gaol that housed over 100 women and children. (As the new prison was being built in response to a finding that the existing facilities were overcrowded, one wonders why the specifications required it to house '40 to 50 women'!)

Within a short time the insanitary and damp conditions, and the over-crowding that began on the first day, were resulting in a steady stream of illnesses and deaths, especially among the children born in the prison. No-one knows exactly how many women and children died, but it is certain that many hundreds did. Life before death was none too special, as the inmates were malnourished, driven hard from morning to night and infested with vermin. Still, at least they were out of the public eye, and weren't in the middle of the city any more…

A genteel public outcry at the number of children dying caused the relocation of the nursery. In fact it was repeatedly relocated, as if it were on the run from public opinion (which it certainly should have been). The reformatory zeal of the authorities consisted in removing the infants from their mothers at nine months, rearing them in the nursery thereafter and then putting them straight in an orphanage. This would have been a successful way of rearing a whole generation of new criminals if more than a few of them had survived. One commentator described the Degraves Street site as the 'Valley of the Shadow of Death.'

The women were not without spirit, however. It became the custom for soldiers to throw food, tobacco and other supplies over the wall once a week, and efforts to prevent the women taking advantage of this were futile. And an indication of the success of attempts to force-feed them religion was that they tried to castrate the chaplain.

The chaplain featured in another famous incident when Governor Sir John Franklin, and his wife Lady Jane Franklin visited the factory to address the inmates. There is some doubt about the truth of this story, but it seems perfectly plausible. Apparently the women listened to Sir John, whom they liked, but muttered and hissed when Lady Franklin began to speak about prison reformer Elizabeth Fry. As Robert Crooke puts it in *The Convict*:

> Her Ladyship, however, a man in petticoats, the Donna Inez of Lord Byron, was disliked by all. Her talents were admitted to be of a very high order, but her love of power and her spirit of meddling and intriguing rendered her a dangerous enemy, and an unsafe friend.

Now that Sir John and Lady Jane had warmed up the crowd, the parson stepped forward to speak. He had hardly started when the whole 300-strong assembly of women turned their backs on him, lifted their skirts and showed him their bare bums, which they then smacked with their hands for good measure.

This was more than the Governor's aide-de-camp could stand. Despite his formal duties, despite his gorgeous ceremonial uniform and the requirement of decorum that he show no emotion, the aide immediately burst out laughing at this barrage of anal applause. Luckily for him, so did

Sir John and Lady Jane Franklin. The parson was not impressed, but humiliation was better than castration.

The Female Factory lasted almost exactly 50 years. After its closure, like many other sandstone structures in Tasmania, it was gradually demolished or fell down by itself. Today, little remains other than some outer walls and the marks of buildings. But what remains is on view; and you can take a tour run from the Island Produce Fudge Factory that offers a comprehensive and well-researched description of the horrors of life in a women's prison in the 19th century. The tour continues around the fudge factory itself and gives an insight into the process of fudge making.

The fudge factory not only occupies the site of the prison; it embraces the spirit of the place. A small and peaceful garden in the grounds is dedicated to the women and children who lived and died there, and continuing archaeological exploration of the site is funded by profits from fudge sales.

Perhaps it's not surprising that the workers look happy. They work for a company that is 'righteous' in the true sense of the word. Perhaps, too, the premises are nowadays less likely to be haunted than they were.

How to get there

The site is in Degraves Street off McRobies Road, South Hobart.

Rory's Story

When Jack Newman (aka Rory Jack Thompson) was found in September 1999, hanged in his cell at Risdon Prison at the age of 57, it was the end of a remarkable and tragic life.

Remarkable, because Dr Rory Thompson was a very clever and successful scientist; tragic, because people who had never heard of him as a scientist knew him as the man who 'murdered his wife and flushed her down the toilet.'

Everyone in Tasmania has an opinion about 'Rory Jack'—and many of the opinions are based on the media coverage of his trial and confinement. His own opinion, too, is worth considering. His book, *Mad Scientist*, tells his life story in his own words.

Rory's early life was in San Diego, California. He was born in 1942 to an American father and a Canadian mother.

At school, he had a difficult time and gave his teachers a difficult time. He didn't start to really achieve at school until Grade 11, when he was taught by a 'real' mathematician/scientist and was grouped with other very bright kids in the honours chemistry and maths classes.

His father had always been distant and his mother turned steadily into an alcoholic, and would eventually try to kill herself. When they split up, he was moved around from place to place—staying with family friends, with his mother, or with his father. Rory already had some trouble socialising due to his quick and often abrasive intelligence, and he now had a fractured home life.

But Grade 11 did a lot for him. He was winning academic prizes, he had friends of similar intellect, and he took up folk dancing and learned to be good at it. He met his first wife Luella through folk dancing, and they were married when he was 17.

Interestingly, even then he was considering emigrating to the Southern Hemisphere because it seemed a safer place in a nuclear war!

His science and maths prizes brought work and scholarship offers from the Navy Electronics Laboratory. He was to work for them while attending San Diego State College, where he graduated in three years, rather than the usual four, by more than doubling his workload in the final year.

He simultaneously left Luella and picked up his doctoral studies at the Massachusetts Institute of Technology. (He would eventually receive a PhD in Fluid Dynamics.) However, he showed an interesting mixture of sex drive and naivety in agreeing some three years after their divorce to have a child with Luella—a daughter, Nuala.

While he was assistant Professor at the University of Oregon, he was beaten up and received serious facial injuries. His anger at the police's attitude and his continuing anger towards his assailant stayed with him, and, he believed, culminated in the death of his second wife, Maureen.

When he went to work at the world-famous Woods Hole Oceanographic Institute in Massachusetts, Luella pursued him there, even persuading him to drive her car from Oregon to Massachusetts for her.

His 'passivity' (his own word) with women is at odds with his direct attitude to people in general. For example, during a seminar on the Isle of Man, he got so bored with the speaker that he opened a window and jumped 2½ metres to the ground. He never seemed to care much 'what people thought'. He slept out under the stars whenever he felt like it; he danced with the Hare Krishna people in the street; he was a Morris dancer; he once told a litterer he was being 'asocial'; he made his first daughter wear a helmet whenever there was any risk of her falling; and his conversational style was direct and sometimes confrontational. He seemed to have no empathy with other people.

Eventually he shook off enough of his passivity to run off to San Diego, where he met Maureen, then a teacher (and according to him, $6000 in debt) at a folk dance in 1974. He was to become her fourth 'husband'.

Rory and Maureen were not legally married when they came to Australia, although they had exchanged vows. He had temporary work at

Monash University and an offer of a tenured position at the University of New South Wales. They landed in Australia arguing already over which job he should take, and she prevailed on him to take an untenured job at the University of Western Australia, because she thought it would have a more pleasant climate. At this time they drew up a legal agreement, which stated among other things that if they ever separated he would have custody of any children they might have.

Around this time, too, Rory began to fantasise about murdering Luella and getting Nuala back from her, which he later claimed was the onset of insanity.

After his time at the University of Western Australia, Rory and Maureen went to Norway so that he could teach at the University of Bergen. They were married in Bergen and their first child, Melody, was born in Norway in 1976.

They had a disastrous visit to the USA, in the course of which he tried to take Nuala away from a 'fat grey woman he didn't recognise' (Luella). His comment: 'Okay, I was unbalanced'. He also fell out with Maureen's family and attempted to leave their house—'…too bad I was not more assertive. If I had left, Maureen would still be alive; I would be working, Melody would have grown up where she lives now, but with her mother…'

Back in Australia, Rory landed a job he liked, with the CSIRO division of Oceanography. He and Maureen began to have serious fights while trying to buy their first house; he felt that she had no grasp of the idea of budgeting, and he was constantly irritated by her readiness to spend more than they could afford.

After a three-month stint as Professor at Florida State University (just so he could say he 'had been a full Professor'), he returned to Australia and the CSIRO.

Their son Rafi was born in 1980, but their relationship was in a bad way. Rory felt that Maureen was behaving irrationally (and she felt the same about him). In 1982 he hit her during a row, and counselling followed. In their whole marriage, he said, he recalled hitting her twice.

A significant incident happened before they came to Tasmania. Over a period of time he killed five of the next-door neighbour's noisy roosters, and got rid of the evidence by burying them…which caused him to fantasise about burying Maureen.

They arrived in Hobart in January 1983, and moved into rented quarters at 234 New Town Road. For the first time in their lives, they now had enough money in the bank to pay cash for a house, and Rory was looking forward to settling down. A Senior Research Scientist with the

CSIRO's Division of Oceanography, he was earning enough to pay 60% income tax.

However, they still weren't getting on—arguing about money, careers, caring, children, self-esteem and all the other things married couples argue about—and once again they drew up one of the notarised agreements that characterised Rory's relationships with women. Under this agreement he paid her $105 a week for 'babysitting'. (Effectively they were now living separate lives a lot of the time, while sometimes coming closer together.)

While he was away at a conference in Perth, Maureen moved out, taking the children to 'a rather dark and small house' she had rented at 99 Hill Street, West Hobart. He believed she had planned this from the start—their furniture had never arrived at New Town Road, but did make it to 99 Hill Street.

Rory now found that although her demands on his money had dropped, she had taken legal steps to make sure he could not spend the money he had in the bank. He felt under attack now. He was accused of domestic violence; Maureen's lawyer had written to Melody's school telling them not to let him visit her there; his visitation rights were under threat; there was an impending court battle for custody; and he often thought of 'making Maureen vanish.'

One Saturday night, when the children were staying with him, he set off (jogging) from New Town Road intending to kill her and bury her, but when in sight of the house he turned around and ran home again to snuggle up with his son.

By now he was sleeping badly and taking a lot of sleeping tablets. He had always tended to read between the words of what people were saying, and this tendency now became more obvious. He felt that lots of people were against him—especially that Maureen was not keeping her signed word about custody, and had perjured herself in having the court order taken out against him. In addition, he and Maureen were simultaneously enduring a lot of stress—a change of job, a move to another state, separation, the death of his mother, a new relationship and the threat of a house move. (Now that there was no longer a 'family' living at New Town Road, the CSIRO wanted it for another family to use.)

When he bought half a sheep to see if he could flush its pieces down the toilet, the end was in sight. The final trigger, according to Rory, was a trivial argument after a trip to the pictures with the children. It seems more likely that the impending court case was what really caused him to act. He tried calling Lifeline, but believed that if he mentioned the temptation to murder, his call would be traced.

While in Sydney to give a talk, he bought a hacksaw and various other tools to dispose of the body. Upon returning to Hobart, he then called Maureen and asked her to put off the court hearing, but she declined. On 10–11 September 1983, he had the children to stay at his house, and once they were in bed (and locked in) he set off for Maureen's house, dressed in a wig and wraparound skirt to conceal his identity, and carrying a bag of tools and a stick. He waited in her garden until she had gone to sleep, then went in to kill her. She woke up; there was a brief struggle in the course of which each hit the other with the stick, and then he strangled her. He believed that she lost consciousness within five seconds of waking up.

Then began his attempt to get rid of the body—to make her disappear. (He later felt that flushing her body parts down the toilet was symbolic and childish. Surely a person with a PhD in fluid dynamics should know that it wasn't going to work.) Having spent all night at this ghastly task, he took the parts he couldn't deal with into the bush above Pottery Road, Lenah Valley, and buried them.

After taking his children swimming the next day, he went to work on Monday and finished a paper—his 50th scientific publication. (He was to have two more published while still in prison.)

When a finger turned up at the sewage works, the police began to close in on him. Even at this stage they appeared to view him as unstable, saying in an interview things like 'Perhaps the bad Rory did such-and-such…'

At first he tried to have the charges dismissed. This in itself would show that he was out of touch with reality, given that over 80 pieces of human tissue had been recovered from Hill Street alone.

He eventually confessed to manslaughter, and at his ensuing trial for murder he started off defending himself. (While he was in remand, Maureen's sister Kathleen and her husband Terry arrived from the USA to take the children and to assure him of their forgiveness.)

At his trial, Rory was to find out for himself the truth of the adage 'a man who defends himself has a fool for a client.' As he had met and been impressed by Pierre Slicer (the duty lawyer at the time, and one whom he considered 'not as slimy as the others'), he asked him to take over the defence.

The verdict of the jury was that he had committed the act as charged but was not guilty by reason of insanity. He was then ordered to be detained in a special institution—the hospital attached to Risdon Prison.

While he was in prison, he was very upset by the attitude of the media towards him. He believed that he was being portrayed as a habitually violent man, a torturer and a mass murderer—none of which he had been charged with. He didn't deny what he had done, but he resented the additional baggage being loaded on him.

In 1990, after he had been in prison for six years, the Mental Health Review Tribunal recommended his release on the grounds that he was no longer insane. Five months later, State Cabinet rejected this decision. Within a couple of months psychiatrist Dr Russell Pargiter resigned from this body, saying that his conscience would not allow him to remain a member of a legally constituted tribunal which had unwittingly become the vehicle of injustice. (The same week, according to Rory, another wife-killer was released as no longer insane. He had also been in prison for six years after stabbing his wife 50 times and trying to throw her body off a bridge.)

Several psychiatric appraisals early in Rory's time in prison showed that although he had a significant personality disorder, he was not mentally ill.

Rory Thompson (or Jack Newman—he changed his name by deed poll in 1994) was recommended for release several times, but was always refused. He was very upset by this, and sought solace by planting a garden of flowers and vegetables at the prison. He was eventually allowed to work unsupervised on his garden outside the prison gates.

On 5 July 1999, in what he described as a 'foolish escape attempt', he walked away from the prison, made his way to Hobart airport and used his credit card to buy a plane ticket. He was arrested on the plane, returned to the prison and refused permission to work unsupervised on his garden.

Finally, after writing a will and transferring money to various members of his family, he hanged himself with a shoelace in his cell on 18 September 1999.

It seems fitting to end with a comment from the final pages of his book—'I am glad to have been alive, though sorry Maureen is not.'

Tasmanian funnel-web spiders

Sydneysiders may take a certain
perverse pride in living with the world's most
dangerous spider—the Sydney funnel-web.
But how many Tasmanians know
that we have a funnel-web of our own?
In fact, we may have two.

F irst, there is the Tasmanian funnel-web, *Atrax vene-natus*, which you may be surprised to hear is very common around Hobart. This is a serious spider—big, black, ugly and aggressive. A large female has a body length of 29 millimetres, and fangs 5 millimetres long that drip venom as it rears up to strike. Its bite is very painful indeed, but unlike the Sydney funnel-web it is not lethal. It makes a black house spider look small, so if you see one you'll know about it.

Then there is (or was) the Cascade funnel-web spider (*Hadronyche Pulvinator*). It has been found only once (in 1925), living in a web-lined burrow in a creek bank in the Cascades area, and it seems likely that its habitat has been destroyed by housing. The Cascade funnel-web is officially extinct—but there may still be hope for it. They said the coelacanth (a species of fish) was extinct until somebody caught one that was 40 million years past its use-by date.

The
Conrad
connection

Two famous Conrads can be
claimed as having Tasmanian connections.
The first is Joseph; the second is Peter.

J oseph Conrad was, of course, a novelist (*Heart of Darkness*,
Nostromo, *Lord Jim*) and a sailor. And if you go to Otago
Bay, near Hobart's Bowen Bridge, you will see what is left
of his connection with the State—the rusting remains of
the barque *Otago*, its ribs pointing up out of the Derwent like those of a
dead animal. The *Otago* was Conrad's first command at sea. Unfortunately
he had long ceased to tread her decks when she fetched up here, but that's
the connection.

Peter Conrad (no relation to Joseph—his real name was Josef
Korzeniowski) has almost the opposite connection. Although most of
Tasmania can tell you who Joseph was, many can point out his ship and a
few have even read his books, Peter is virtually unknown on these shores.

Yet he is the author of 15 books, a broadcaster, a lecturer, a Rhodes
Scholar, a former Fellow of All Souls College, Oxford, and a minor
celebrity in England and America. And he was born and raised in

Glenorchy. (In fact, as a child he starred in the film of Nan Chauncy's *They Found a Cave*.) He even went to the same school as movie star, Errol Flynn and legendary cameraman, Neil Davis—Hobart High.

Conrad saw Tasmania as a place to be escaped from, as a life to be left behind, and describes himself as having been 'born' on London's Waterloo Bridge at the age of 20. Curiously, this is the same Waterloo Bridge where the remains of another Tasmanian, Mr Radcliff (see 'The coroner who came to a sticky end' on page 142) had been found 100 years before. Conrad has, despite his eagerness to escape, written a book (*Down Home: Revisiting Tasmania*) about his early life in Tasmania and about what Tasmania means to him at his present remove of time and distance. He was criticised in Tasmania for his portrayal of the State in *Down Home*, but he has lately begun to view his early years here as something other than a gaol term. Maybe he has realised that working-class England in the 1950s, although romanticised by distance, would not have been a much better place to grow up. Much of what he wrote about Tasmania at the time, although bleak in outlook, was quite valid.

Peter Conrad is over 50 now, and the mind that has cut such a swathe through the English cultural world will eventually start to lose its edge. When it does, who knows? Perhaps he'll come back to Tasmania to retire.

How to get there

Conrad's childhood home, as described in *Down Home*, is at 107 Renfrew Circle, Goodwood (the other end of the Bowen Bridge from Otago Bay)—although the letterbox he mentions, which was a miniature copy of the actual house, has now been replaced.

Neil. Davis, frontline cameraman

In a small garden in the street outside the Sorell
Council Chambers there is a stone with a plaque
on it inscribed: 'In memory of: Geoffrey Crocker Davis,
Manfred Weil, Beatrice Burdon, Edith Hayton
and Ada Irene Barwick who lost their lives in
the tragic bushfires on 7th February 1967 which
devastated the whole Sorell community.'

The first-named victim, Geoffrey Crocker Davis, better
known as Geoff Davis, was killed in a firestorm while
fighting the bushfires of 1967 (see page 8). He was one
of 62 people who died in those fires. What would have pleased him more
than most parents was that his son Neil considered him a hero.

Neil Davis knew exactly what a hero was. He saw them in action every
day of his life. By any normal definition he was one. At the time of his
father's death he was a combat cameraman covering the Vietnam War, with
occasional side trips to other breaking news stories, such as the fall of
Indonesia's General Sukarno.

The Davis family home was at Belle Vue, on Pawleena Road, Sorell (where his family moved from Nala after his great-grandfather dropped dead outside the Gordon Highlander Hotel while running and drinking his way from Hobart to Bream Creek). Although Neil Davis no longer lived in Tasmania, his boyhood as a farmer's son and his early days in the wild beauty of Tasmania gave him a sympathy with the rural scene—as well as a matter-of-fact acceptance of life and death that was to be useful to him in the jungles of South-East Asia.

Davis spent most of his time with the native troops—the ARVN or Army of the Republic of Vietnam —for a complicated mix of reasons. He felt safer with them, he liked the way they operated, he had lived like them in his childhood, and he felt that their story wasn't being fairly told by others.

In the hard, dangerous, competitive world of the combat cameraman, Neil Davis was acknowledged by his peers as the best. But he didn't just drop into it. He had learned his craft first at the Sorell School, where he was a top (if fairly wayward) primary student, then at Hobart High School, and then at the Tasmanian Film Unit. At the Film Unit he learned a lot of important lessons—the art of conserving film and keeping up a good ratio of usable footage to shot footage, and the importance of keeping accurate and reliable records of activities and finances. After 13 years with the Unit (under the tutelage of another Tasmanian legend, Jack Thwaites), he left its Bathurst Street premises (now a pet shop) to join the ABC in 1961.

His horizons expanded rapidly in 1964 when he went to Singapore as a staff cameraman for Visnews, and very shortly afterwards he found himself covering the confrontation in the jungles of Borneo.

Over the next 20 years he would see action in Indochina, the Middle East, Malaysia, Indonesia, the Philippines, Bangladesh, Angola, the Sudan, Iraq... Wherever a story was breaking, Davis was there, talking to his myriad contacts, arranging interviews, on patrol with the front line troops, advising new journalists on the local scene, chasing women and drinking and betting endlessly.

He had contacts at every level. He rubbed shoulders with Sukarno, General Ky, General Thieu, Prince Sihanouk, General de Gaulle, Ninoy Aquino and a hundred other dignitaries—and he brought a studied irreverence to the rubbing. He even drew on his contacts sufficiently to cross the lines and film the Viet Cong in action—and in one case in Cambodia went into Communist territory not to film, but to ask for the release of a fellow journalist who had been captured.

Davis might have remained relatively unknown to many, except his media colleagues, had David Bradbury not made a film about him called

Frontline (1980). Bradbury set out to make a film that was just about combat cameramen, but it quickly became apparent to him that in many ways there was only one. The summary of a cameraman's work is the lasting images —and Davis had more lasting images than anyone else.

He was the one who stood in the grounds of the Presidential Palace in Saigon on 30 April 1975 and filmed the first North Vietnamese tank knocking down the gates. He was the one who kept his camera rolling while General Loan summarily executed a Viet Cong soldier in the street with his pistol.

Seriously wounded half a dozen times, he was thought by his colleagues to be invincible; but less than five years after the film was made, Davis was killed, at the age of 51, in a Bangkok street while filming one of Thailand's abortive coup attempts. His camera kept rolling even then.

David is remembered in the Sorell Library by the Neil Davis Collection—a collection of books donated by the Rotary Club of Sorell—and by the Neil Davis Award, which is presented by the Rotary Club to outstanding students in schools throughout the municipality.

Although his father Geoff is buried in Sorell, Neil was cremated and most of his ashes are in Bangkok. Plaques to both Geoff and Neil can be found in the Memorial Wall behind St Georges Church. Neil in fact has two, and some of his ashes are behind one of them.

Neil was also the posthumous winner of a Humanitarian Pater, an award presented by the media for significant service to humanity. Other recipients include Bob Geldof and Radio Veritas, Manila (the Philippines' 'Voice of the Voiceless' for 2½ years after the Aquino assassination until forcibly silenced by Marcos's troops). As well as his ability and achievements as a correspondent, the citation highlights his 'compassion and generosity to disadvantaged children, refugees and other victims of war.'

How to get there

The house at Nala where Neil Davis was born no longer stands, but a drive through the area is interesting. In Oatlands, take the C312 for Parattah; after 6 kilometres take the C310 and drive 4 kilometres to Andover. Then turn left on the C309, drive 2.5 kilometres and you're in Nala. You can continue on this road and drive in a loop back to the Midland Highway via the C307.

The old house at Belle Vue in Sorell has also gone.

Triple tragedy
at Cygnet

In a town with two roads
bearing the names 'Silver Hill Road'
and 'Golden Valley Road', you might
reasonably expect to find mines. Cygnet
is not generally thought of as a major
gold mining area, but it did
once have gold mines.

One of these, on Mount Mary, was the scene of a triple tragedy in 1898. A leadlight window in the Cygnet Catholic Church mentions two of the victims, but not the third. (He was an Anglican, and is buried in the Anglican churchyard.)

On the morning of 30 March 1898, Edmond Dillon and the 15-year-old Edward Ryan were working together at the Mount Mary gold mine. Using a windlass, Ryan lowered Dillon (on a crossbar tied to a rope) down the 18-metre mine shaft. When things went quiet down below, Ryan suspected something was wrong and ran for help. (The mine is not far from Cygnet.) With a policeman to man the windlass, Ryan lowered himself down the rope to his friend. Constable Hall, at the surface, heard him call to be brought up, but the crossbar came up without him.

James Wicks the blacksmith had by now arrived, and volunteered to be lowered into the shaft. Despite suggestions that he tie himself to the rope, he refused—possibly to save time. Like the others, he died down there, from what was later discovered to be asphyxiation.

Eventually, thanks to further acts of heroism by several people, the bodies were brought back to the surface. Some people who tried to go down were brought back unconscious; luckily no-one else died. James Boyd recovered the first two bodies; Herbert Mills the third (after Boyd came up unconscious from his third attempt.)

The inscription on the gravestone of James Wicks (paid for by the people of Cygnet) says all that needs to be said:

In Memory of W James E Wicks
Who lost his life in the Mount Mary Mine
Trying to save others
March 30 1898
Aged 24
Greater love hath no man than this,
That a man lay down his life for his friends

How not to get there

The Mount Mary Mine is disused today. Because it is a vertical shaft, it is potentially dangerous, so we do not recommend that you go looking for it.

A
quiet
stroll
40 metres
in the air

When it first opened in mid-2001,
Forestry Tasmania's Tahune Forest AirWalk
was probably Tasmania's most immediately
successful attraction.

S o what's it doing in a book called *Secret Tasmania*? Just this—going into the bush, and looking at trees and rivers isn't everyone's cup of tea. So you could go through life thinking you didn't want to see the AirWalk, and miss out on a unique experience.

It takes about an hour and a quarter of leisurely driving to get there from Hobart—'there' being about 30 kilometres west of Geeveston in the Tahune Forest Reserve.

There are plenty of signs pointing to the AirWalk, so you shouldn't miss it. On the way, there are a number of short and charming side trips you can make to attractions which are mostly just off the road. These include the Look In Lookout, which takes you into a logging scene from long ago, with old machinery painted in garish colours and the remains of an old wooden tram track. Just up the road is the Arve River Picnic Area, beautifully sited by a typical southwest river. You can also gaze up at The Big Tree—an 87-metre tall Swamp Gum—and visit the West Creek Lookout, which is a kind of mini-AirWalk. At the end of a 'gangway' extending from the roadside you find yourself looking from a great height at a breathtaking profusion of greenery on the other side of the valley. Rainforest at the bottom of the valley gradually gives way, via an Escheresque patchwork of huge manferns and sassafras trees, to eucalypt forest at the top.

When you get to the AirWalk, you pay to get in. You then set off on an easy walk of a few hundred (concreted) metres, that takes you over the Huon River and up across the slope where the AirWalk stands. It's an imposing sight—tubular steel towers, like something out of *War of the Worlds*, carry the slender walkway right through the forest canopy—and when you've seen it snaking overhead you wonder how you're going to get up onto it.

You needn't worry; the path takes you well up the slope, and the AirWalk launches out almost horizontally from there. (There is also a road leading to it, so those who can't cope with the path can get alternative transport to the AirWalk itself.)

Walking on the AirWalk is actually easier than walking on the ground in the bush; it's probably even safer, too, as you are walking on a flat floor between 'fences' on either side. Under your feet is a grid through which you can see all the way to the forest floor, 40–45 metres down; so if you have a problem with heights, don't look! The climax of the AirWalk experience—half a kilometre of it—is probably the cantilevered viewing platform that reaches out (with little visible means of support) towards the confluence of the Huon and Picton rivers. Taking photographs from this can be a frustrating experience if anyone is walking out from the main structure, as the viewing platform goes gently up and down with each stride...

Even walking back down the path to the restaurant (part of the 21st-century wilderness experience!) is interesting. Because now you can look up at the tiny figures peering over the edge of the AirWalk and think 'I've just been up there!'

How to get there

In Geeveston, take the C632 and follow the AirWalk signs.

Wild
West and
Wilderness

Woolnorth

The far northwest of Tasmania is a wild,
spectacular and inhospitable place. The weather
here comes straight off the Southern Ocean
and it's hard to stand up straight if you're
unfortunate enough to be on the coastline
when a high wind is blowing.

I t is a land of superlatives. The last four Tasmanian tigers
ever captured were caught at 'Woolnorth', for example.
Here the baseline weather monitoring station at Cape
Grim has officially identified the cleanest air in the world. Here, too, is one
of Tasmania's largest farms, the 22 100-hectare 'Woolnorth', and on it a
titanic shearing shed and the largest circular dairy in the Southern
Hemisphere. The dairy (one of several on the property) consists of a vast
building housing an enormous turntable on which the cows stand in a
wide circle, rotating gently towards the exit while being milked and fed.

It's not easy to get a look at any of this. The Van Diemen's Land
Company, owners of 'Woolnorth', are fairly secretive. You have to pay, and
pay handsomely, for a guided tour. However, the tour is spectacular and
informative in the extreme—the sheer scale of the property beggars the
imagination (of a Tasmanian, at least) and the barbecue lunch is as good as
you'll get anywhere. Lunch is at the 'Top House', a residence in a com-
manding position on a hill built in the shape of an aeroplane by a previous
manager who loved flying.

Woolnorth Point is the most northerly point on mainland Tasmania, and when you stand on it, it's easy to see why Bass Strait is such a ships' graveyard. Several currents meet at this point (the number has been placed as high as seven), and the sea is generally rough and unpredictable. Not far off is Trefoil Island, scene of the Kay tragedy (see 'Tragedy at Trefoil Island' on page 60), and just along the coast is the wreck of the *Colliboi* (commemorated in the Bridge Hotel in Smithton). A few kilometres south of Woolnorth Point, near Cape Grim, is Suicide Bay, where a large group of Tasmanian Aboriginal people allegedly jumped to their deaths rather than face capture by European settlers. ('Allegedly', because it would be equally easy to imagine them being driven over the cliffs.)

'Woolnorth' is more than just a pastoral property—it's a whole community, made up of a number of large, self-managing sheep, beef cattle and (since 1994) dairy farms. It even has its own miniature museum.

Although it has certainly moved with the times, 'Woolnorth' is one of the oldest properties in the State, and is still operating under its original charter from King George IV.

How to get there

Leave Smithton on the C215—the Montagu Road. It's about a 25-kilometre drive, probably through steady, misty rain, before you see the impressive stone 'Woolnorth' gateposts. If you're taking an individual tour, you leave your vehicle here and your guide drives out to pick you up. If you've come on an organised bus tour, then you do the tour in your own bus.

Tragedy at Trefoil Island

Just 5 kilometres off the wild coast
of Cape Grim is 100 hectares of superb
sheep pasture fertilised for millennia by
the droppings of millions of mutton-birds.
It is known as Trefoil Island.

T he name comes from the island's resemblance to a three-pronged leaf. Leased by the Van Diemen's Land Company at Woolnorth to a succession of tenant farmers who used it to run their sheep, this lonely island was the scene in 1895 of a family tragedy that hardly bears thinking about.

The end of October 1895 saw the arrival on Trefoil of Albert Kay of Forest, his young wife Maria (who was pregnant) and their eight children Walter, Belinda, Albert, Lydia, Janey, Wintena, Sarah and Robert. They had arranged for the *May Queen* to pick them up in a month's time, in late November. Albert and Maria ran some 400 sheep on Trefoil, and were in the habit of spending several weeks at a time on the island with their whole family to shear their sheep and go mutton-birding.

Unfortunately, not long after their arrival, something—possibly a problem with the pregnancy—caused Albert and Maria to leave for the mainland. They took with them their eldest son, 16-year-old Walter, and the four-year-old Sarah. Leaving the remaining six children in the care of the eldest, 13-year-old Belinda, they assured her that Albert and Walter would be back that day or early the next, and set off in the island's dinghy to row across the narrow strait to Woolnorth. This was known to be a dangerous passage, with strong currents, rushing tides and many shoals.

They never reached Woolnorth alive. The six children, the youngest less than two years old, watched in horror as the dinghy was swamped. None of those in the boat could swim except Albert, and as he was partly disabled ('practically a cripple', the *Wellington Times* said with astonishing callousness) he was a poor swimmer. The children's parents, their older brother and their little sister drowned in front of them.

The Kay children were now alone, not only in the world, but on a Bass Strait island. By the time the *May Queen* arrived to pick up what they thought was the whole family, Belinda and the others had survived for six weeks on their own by eating sheep killed with an axe. The horror of those six weeks can hardly be imagined, but it is easy to guess at the resourcefulness of the 13-year-old who led the children through it. Unfortunately, Belinda suffered a nervous breakdown after her rescue and never really recovered.

How to get there

You can't, unless you take a tour of Woolnorth, in which case you can see it from Cape Grim.

Darwin
Crater:
the invisible impact

In an island as mountainous as Tasmania,
complete with extinct volcanoes, glaciation
of all kinds and nearly every other feature of
a geologists' playground, it would be a major
disappointment if we didn't have a
substantial meteorite crater.

U ntil quite recently it was thought that we'd have to do without unless something turned up from space; but it is now apparent that we do have one. It has been known for many years that some of the Tasmanian Aboriginal people used glass as a cutting tool. Some examples have been found in the prehistoric Kutikina Cave on the Lower Franklin River. They didn't get it from bottles. Where they did get it from was not so clear, although the men who lived on the Jukes–Darwin mining field (north of Kelly Basin in Macquarie Harbour) found a good deal of the same apparently natural glass in the course of their operations. Looking at its colour and texture, they decided that it was 'petrified kelp'. Although this was an educated guess, it was not correct.

The glass was in the form of tektites—'beads' that have solidified from globules of material melted by a blast of some kind—although it was less regular in shape than many other tektites.

The true origin of the glass and the blast that created it were unknown until 1974, when road-building activities exposed more of it. A core was drilled to the southeast of Queenstown, and it became clear that underneath the rainforest there was a depression filled with sediment.

Further geophysical research showed that the now-apparent (but hardly visible) impact crater was at least 200 metres deep, and 1 kilometre across, and the 'strewnfield' (the area over which the glass was scattered) covered some 400 square kilometres.

The crater is in a slight depression, but cannot be seen, firstly because it has no rim (the raised edge on three sides does not result from the impact), secondly because it is full of sediment, and thirdly because the vegetation is extremely dense. (It took 100 man-hours with chainsaws to clear a 2500-metre track just wide enough for survey lines.)

Nonetheless, something from space crashed into the ground here three-quarters of a million years ago. The likeliest suspects are a meteorite or a comet. Whatever it was, it has been conservatively estimated as weighing several hundred tonnes. The 50 tonnes of melted glass that it blasted out is by far the largest quantity on earth from an impact of this size.

It's known as Darwin Crater because it's close to Mount Darwin. In fact, Mount Darwin (1031 metres above sea level), to the northwest, is where much of the glass is found. This seems to suggest that the meteorite came in from the southeast on a trajectory that would have taken it close to the present site of Hobart.

How lucky we are that we weren't here to see it land; and what a pity we can't see it now!

How to get there

There is a rough track leading to Darwin Crater from the Franklin River Road. Both are marked on 1:25 000 maps of the area. However, unless you're an experienced bushwalker it might be best to settle for viewing some samples of Darwin glass at 'Shorty's Private Collection' at 22 Shaw Street, Zeehan. (Entry is by gold coin donation.)

First vehicles to Zeehan

Nowadays you can drive from Waratah to
Zeehan with very little effort, if you take the highway.
Try doing it down the coast, however, and you'll
find it a lot more challenging.

T he first time any motor vehicle went from Waratah to Zeehan was in 1924, and the vehicles were motor-cycles—750cc Indian Scouts. No springs, no shock absorbers. The riders were Fred Smithies (a legend in Tasmanian bush-walking circles) and Bill King (an equally legendary photographer and transport pioneer). It's an indication of the times that they called each other 'Mr Smithies' and 'Mr King'. Mr King, the Indian motorcycle dealer in Launceston at the time, supplied and modified the bikes. The West Coast of Tasmania is still, capital-R, Rugged even today. The weather comes from the Antarctic, the waves from South America and the winds from the Roaring Forties. The locals eat barbed wire for breakfast. And there are great lumps of the West Coast that still don't have any roads.

> Tasmania, generally speaking, is well known as a motorist's paradise, with its wonderful network of good metalled roads connecting, with one notable exception, practically all the settled and most of the unsettled parts of the island.

The notable exception Mr Smithies is talking about is the West Coast, accessible in 1924 only by various railways.

The road at this stage went only to 24 miles beyond Waratah, and it was from here that Smithies and King proposed to 'break through to Zeehan by Motor Cycle'. In planning for their trip they discovered that the locals were keen to point out the difficulties ahead of them; he suspected that they were being written off as a 'pair of harmless lunatics'.

The first job was to contact Mr Jack Ahrberg, who lived in the only house on this section of the coast and ran an infrequent ferry service on the Pieman River. The mail was irregular, but they managed to make an arrangement with Ahrberg to meet them at Corinna with a boat to carry themselves and their motorcycles down to Pieman Heads. On 16 February 1924 they set off from Launceston, reaching Waratah at midday and Whyte River, 11 miles further on, later in the day. Here they spent the night.

For the first 10 miles the next day the road was good, but then it ended abruptly and they were forced to follow a miners' pack track.

> We were not long in meeting trouble, the track in some places being rutted out by the heavy rains, banks had slipped down so that in some places we were pushed out onto the extreme edge of precipitous slopes, winding round the sides of deep ravines...

Then came Long Plains, with Mount Sunday on one side and the huge gorges that guard the Meredith Range on the other:

> On this bright sunny day it has a beauty all its own, but it is easy to imagine it under other circumstances, and one can picture the hardy pioneers of those early days battling their way through the roaring blizzards which must at times sweep across these plains.

A bullock's-head signpost pointed the way to Savage River and they rode on, 'conscious all the while of a feeling of almost sacrilege at disturbing the vast solitude with the crackling exhaust of unmuffled engines for the first time since the creation of the World'.

Crackling exhausts weren't the only thing that disturbed the solitude—the crunch of metal on scrub and occasionally the thud of a body on the ground must have added to the effect. Bill King, for example, grew tired of lifting his motorcycle over fallen trees, so he started charging his front wheel over them and then moving his feet from the footboards to the tree trunk to allow the back wheel to jump over. Fred Smithies was not, apparently, so skilful: 'Endeavouring to emulate Mr King's example my first effort was a failure—the front wheel striking the log slightly on an angle and, swerving aside, I was deposited in the nearby scrub.'

The next line of defence was a tank-trap of blackberry bushes covering the track to a depth of up to a metre and hanging on either side like curtains. 'Charging' was, they decided, the only way through—the result being that when they emerged on the banks of the Pieman River they looked like escapees from an abattoir. Now where was Jack Ahrberg?

To our great delight our hail was answered by a gunshot close at hand.

Jack Ahrberg had never seen a motorcycle before, having lived mostly at sea or in his lonely lookout at Pieman Heads.

Those who have never attempted to get two motor-cycles into a 14-foot boat and still leave room for three passengers with sufficient space for rowing can hardly appreciate the difficulty this presented.

It was 3.20 a.m. that night when they reached the Heads and Ahrberg's shack. At 3.40 a.m. it started to rain, and continued to do so for a week. As a result they were there for nine days, waiting for the streams to go down. (As a result too, they ate Ahrberg out of house and home; so when they did set off for Zeehan, he came too, to get supplies, on horseback.)

They occupied the time partly in exploring the area and partly in repairing a dead outboard motor which someone had given Ahrberg years before. When it was fixed he tried it out immediately, giving them an opportunity for a better look at the unique beauty of the Pieman River (which they had previously seen only in the dark, in a state of near exhaustion).

When the rains finally abated, they were able to set off for Zeehan; but first they had to cross several miles of buttongrass plains, 'and very rough going it proved'. The biggest problem, apparently, was that a motorcycle would occasionally leap over the top of a clump of buttongrass and land on it with both wheels hanging in the air. Indian Scouts were never famous for being easy motorcycles to lift.

Then they had to run the gauntlet of the beaches. On the first of these, the Four Mile Beach (today known as Ahrberg Bay) they covered as much distance in 10 minutes as they had in two hours over buttongrass plains. But the beaches had a nasty shock in store, in the form of the 'drawback'.

This is a phenomenon peculiar to these exposed ocean beaches. One moment the breakers are a few hundred metres out, minding their own business; the next, they come rushing in all the way up the beach like killer whales; then, just as suddenly, they retreat again. This bizarre behaviour has its advantages when you want to cross a creek—and there were three on the Four Mile Beach.

The drill, apparently, is to race out after the retreating waves to cross where the creek fans out across the sand, and then go hell for leather up the beach on the other side. Unfortunately the movement of the breakers is a tad unpredictable. As Fred Smithies says:

> ...the thought of negotiating the three streams...had provided us with certain anticipatory thrills for a week or more.

They got away with it and soon returned to 'the awful buttongrass'—so bad and so boggy were the buttongrass plains that they were delighted to come on a stretch of corduroy road (made from logs laid crosswise in the dirt). 'This at least was solid and we could put up with the terrific vibration and jolting so long as our heads remained attached to our bodies'.

At Granville Farm they were faced with the choice of continuing down the coast to Trial Harbour or turning inland along 29 kilometres of the Granville Horse Tram track to Zeehan. They chose the tram track, but soon discovered that in some places the horses had kicked all the ballast out from between the sleepers. As the sleepers were 600 millimetres apart it was sometimes impossible to ride, so they put the bikes up on the 100-millimetre wooden rails and walked alongside with the engines running.

Two miles along the tram track they arrived at North Icemakirk, where they spent the night at Mr Gordon's store. Here too, they said goodbye to Jack Ahrberg, who loaded his horse with provisions and set off into the night, walking alongside his horse, for the 35-kilometre tramp back to his shack.

Next day they rode the remaining 26 kilometres to Zeehan, where they were warmly welcomed—not surprisingly, since it was the first time the inhabitants had had to welcome a motor vehicle.

A final word about the adventure from Fred Smithies:

> The scenery throughout was magnificent and some day I hope that this section of our beautiful Island will be properly opened up and appreciated by thousands instead of the comparatively few who have an opportunity of viewing it under present conditions.

Unfortunately (or perhaps fortunately) it's still a fairly well-kept secret.

How to get there

You can follow their wheel tracks (approximately) by driving from Waratah to Savage River on the B23. Then the C247 takes you to Corinna, where you cross the Pieman River by car ferry. From here you can drive to Zeehan on the C249.

A modest
genius

Wherever you look in Australia, you will
find things called 'Flinders'—mountain ranges,
streets, railway stations, and our own Flinders Island.
They are all, of course, named after Matthew Flinders,
explorer, navigator and cartographer *extraordinaire*;
yet he was such a modest man that
none were named by him.

His name is often mixed up with that of George Bass (after whom he recommended that Governor Hunter name Bass Strait), and as a result his achievements tend to be a bit veiled. How many of us know, for example, that the name 'Australia' itself was first applied by Flinders? At the end of the 18th century it was known as either New Holland or Terra Australis—neither of them glittering examples of the namer's art. 'Australia' seemed to him a natural name, and one in line with the names of the other four continents at the time (Asia, Europe, Africa and The Americas).

It was to New Holland that he sailed on his first voyage to the Southern Hemisphere, as timekeeper/midshipman aboard the *Providence*, under Captain Bligh (yes, *the* Captain Bligh). Their first Australian port of call was Adventure Bay, Bruny Island. Flinders was there when Bligh revisited the first apple tree in the Southern Hemisphere, which he had planted three years before.

At this time (1792) it was thought that Van Diemen's Land was just a southerly extension of Terra Australis, and the shape of the continent itself was only partly and vaguely known. It must have been a depressing prospect for ships'captains and navigators to see maps where coastlines tailed off into nothingness.

On his next voyage from England to Australia, the ship's surgeon was one George Bass. When the pair reached Botany Bay they set off together in the tiny *Tom Thumb* (less than 2½ metres long!) to begin exploring the Australian coastline. Bass's appetite for exploration was thoroughly whetted by this voyage, by a subsequent one with Flinders on *Tom Thumb II* (not much bigger) and by a trip into what is now Bass Strait in a 5-metre whaleboat. (It was on this trip that Bass noticed the size of the long southwesterly swell, and deduced that it must be coming from the Indian Ocean.)

Flinders' next Tasmanian trip was as a lieutenant, with the schooner *Francis*, to salvage cargo from the wreck of the *Sydney Cove* on the Furneaux Islands.

Governor Hunter of New South Wales, impressed by the courage and skill of Bass and Flinders, then gave them the 25-ton sloop *Norfolk*. (If you want to see how big that is, there is a full-size replica, built by Bern Cuthbertson. She must, all the same, have seemed palatial after the *Tom Thumb*.) Their mission was to sail right around Van Diemen's Land, if possible, and thereby establish whether there was a strait between it and the 'mainland'.

This they did, naming a great many coastal features on the way that today we take for granted—Cape Barren Island, Great Island (now Flinders Island), Hunter Island, Table Cape, Rocky Cape, Circular Head, Three Hummock Island, Trefoil Island and so on. Flinders' remarks about the little-frequented West Coast were hideously prophetic—'Judging from appearances, the West Coast of Van Diemen's Land is as dreary and inhospitable a shore as has yet been discovered...' He goes on to predict large numbers of shipwrecks if 'dull-sailing' ships get too close to this coast.

When he returned to England this time, Flinders managed to meet up with Sir Joseph Banks, and to ask for his help in putting together a survey voyage to chart the whole coastline of Australia.

So it was with the rank of Commander, and with a crew that included both his own brother Samuel and his relative the young John (later Sir John) Franklin, that Matthew Flinders sailed his new ship, the *Investigator*, back into Australian waters for his final voyage of discovery. (*Lady Nelson* was to accompany them, to explore river systems with her flat bottom, but

Flinders sent her home as she was sailing badly and had lost her anchors. He also had a low opinion of her as a sailing boat, which is at variance with Governor Macquarie's description of her as 'the best little sea boat I ever sailed in' (see page 12).

By the time this voyage was over, Flinders had charted almost the entire coastline of Australia with such accuracy that some of his charts are still used today; and the skills he used had been honed in that earlier circumnavigation of the stormy waters off Tasmania.

Footnote: It took Flinders many years to get back to England. First he was shipwrecked and marooned. Then he was captured in Mauritius and imprisoned as a suspected spy by the French. His imprisonment added seven years to his separation from the wife he had married just before leaving for Australia. He died (probably of a venereal disease as well as from the privations he had suffered) in England at the age of 40, the day after he received the first copy of *A Voyage to Terra Australis* from his publisher. This splendid work, comprising his meticulous charts and two volumes of description, is a classic of exploration and cartography, and a superb facsimile edition of it (in a large red plush case) can be seen in the Tasmaniana Collection of the State Library of Tasmania in Murray Street, Hobart.

The Franklins' journey

At the top end of Lenah Valley Road, Hobart,
among the trees by the roadside, you'll find a
miniature Greek temple, the Ancanthe (a Greek
word meaning 'vale of flowers'). The area where
it stands is now called Ancanthe Park. It was built
to the specifications of Lady Jane Franklin as
a museum and library. It is now occasionally
used as an art gallery.

L ady Jane is well known, not only as the wife of the
Arctic explorer and Governor of Tasmania Sir John
Franklin, but in her own right. She is credited with
being a prime mover in changing the name 'Van Diemen's Land' to
'Tasmania'. She gave her name to the Jane Franklin Hall residential college
in Elboden Street, and also to the town of Franklin, which she virtually
founded by leasing parcels of her own land to poor farmers. She is also mentioned elsewhere in this book (see 'From drudgery to fudgery' on page 38)
for a notorious, and possibly mythical, occurrence on a visit she made to the
Female Factory. She was viewed in different ways by different people—
some finding her down-to-earth and approachable, others the reverse.

Certainly she preferred good company to the 'compulsory company' that was often the lot of a governor's wife; and she was far from being a typical gentleman's wife, showing an independence that was well ahead of her time.

Another exploit of her husband and herself was their famous walk from Hobart to Macquarie Harbour in 1842. They did this to see if there was any land in the southwest that was suitable for immediate settlement, and also so that the governor could familiarise himself with 'this obscure portion of the island.' It was a courageous effort on her part, particularly considering her fear of snakes. (In a moment of lunacy she had tried to rid the island of them, and paid out £600 in one-shilling bounties for dead snakes.)

It took the party two days to reach Hamilton, and two more to get to Ellendhu, on the Ouse River. Within a week they were almost on the edge of civilisation, at 'Marlboro Township', which their diarist David Burn describes as 'doubtless destined at no very distant date to take honourable rank amid the country towns of Tasmania.' (It hasn't done so yet, and had at that stage only one cottage. It was in the Bronte Park region.)

Their next stop was on April Fool's Day at what is now Derwent Bridge, where two bark huts had been built for them in advance. They strolled up from here to look at Lake St Clair, and Mount Olympus above it (named by the former Surveyor-General; a 'singular perversion of taste', says Mr Burn, 'to give a Greek title to the hill, and a Scotch one to the water.')

The eight members of the official party who were continuing set off the next day across the plains to the foot of Mount King William. They were Sir John and Lady Jane, his aide-de-camp Lieutenant Bagot, a surgeon called Milligan, Mr Burn (the writer), Mr Calder (a surveyor), Corporal Boyle and 'Stewart' (Lady Jane's female companion). There were also 20 convict servants with them, but they seem to have been viewed as not really members of the party. Nonetheless, four of them were carrying Lady Jane, where possible, in a palanquin.

At Mount King William, Mr Calder found a human skeleton. This they assumed was of a Macquarie Harbour escapee (who had nearly made it!)

From here on their progress can be marked by the names they gave to features along the way, many of which are still used—Burns Plains stretched out ahead of them and took them (via 'Fatigue Hill', a name bestowed by the non-existent convicts) to Calders Lookout.

Their next stop was 13 kilometres further on, at Wombat Glen, which seems to have rivalled the present-day Bakers Beach for wombat numbers. The way had been well prepared for them, and this was their second food depot. That night they had some heavy rain; it is a demonstration of their equipment level that they guessed it to be 25 millimetres of rain from the amount of it they found in a candlestick next morning! After crossing the Loddon River and Loddon Plains, and making another overnight stop within sight of Frenchmans Cap, they were stuck for nine days in 'tempestuous…wind and rain.'

It took them another day to reach the Franklin River, which was naturally running very high after all the rain. They spent four days building a double dugout canoe to cross it. Unfortunately one of the convicts, Mumford, managed to put his eye out with a branch while cutting wood, and was in a lot of pain for the rest of the journey. They camped again on the Western Plains, having named the Pig Trough en route. Burn wrote, 'We were now seven miles from the *Breeze*' [the schooner they were to meet].

The next day they reached the Gordon River, at Expectation Reach, which Burn called 'one of the most perfectly lovely land-locked basins I ever beheld,' and very gratefully met up with the 28-tonner, *Breeze*.

A trip which they had expected to finish in eight days had actually taken 21 days. They now spent an extra week in exploration and in trying to leave the deserted Macquarie Harbour (which Burn described as 'somewhat of the moistest'). A combination of calms and storms kept them inside Hells Gates, the treacherous mouth of Macquarie Harbour, until at last the conditions were right and they could leave for Hobart.

On the way into Hobart after the usual stormy passage around the southwest coast, they heard that the cutter *Vansittart* had just arrived from Launceston. It would eventually set sail for Macquarie Harbour to pick up the remains of the rescue team that had been sent out after the Franklins!

This rescue team had an epic all of its own, and a much more serious one than the Franklins'. Twenty men reached the Franklin River about a fortnight after the Franklin party had left. Here, 12 of them left as much food as they could spare and set off back to Hobart. Two more would follow later. The remaining six took two days to cross the river (again in a hand-built canoe), and on reaching Macquarie Harbour built huge fires in the hope of attracting the attention of the long-gone *Breeze*.

They soon realised that they were marooned, and decided to walk around the southwest coast without dogs, guns or, after a while, food. They found so much debris from shipwrecks that they began to think the *Breeze* had gone down, and after 11 days found their way blocked by a fast-flowing river, which they were in no condition to cross. On their way back to Macquarie Harbour they scraped together a few meals from a rotting bullock, an equally rotten whale and whatever else they could forage.

At Macquarie Harbour there was at least food—potatoes and cabbages left over from the convict days—so they filled their stomachs and four of them set off to walk back overland to Lake St Clair. Two they had to leave behind for later rescue by ship because they were very lame.

The rescuers were themselves rescued 80 kilometres from Lake St Clair, with no food left. They had set out after the Franklins nearly two months before, and had had only five days of good weather. (Burn, who had travelled about a month ahead of the rescue party, would not have realised that he was being optimistic when he commented that it seemed to rain 'about three days out of four'!)

How to get there

Following in the footsteps of the Franklins would be a major expedition. Although there are tracks into the area, in many places the tracks do not follow where they went. Travelling off the tracks is at best difficult, at worst dangerous. We do not recommend it.

The less ambitious traveller might want to have a look at the Ancanthe in Lenah Valley, and at Sir John's statue in Hobart's Franklin Square.

Tasmania's
remotest
museum

You may well have been to the ski fields at
Mount Mawson and endured the organised
and modernised chaos that is commercial downhill
skiing. However, you probably don't know that not
too far away there is a time warp—a place where
the skis don't have garish logos on them; where
the construction materials have mostly been found
nearby; and where your coffee is not bought, but
made (provided you've carried it in with you).

U nless you're a cross-country skier it's easier to reach
the Twilight Tarn Hut in the summer than during
the winter ski season. A fairly easy track, much of it
boardwalk, leads you up the ski slopes towards Tarn Shelf, where you bear
right along the broad ledge with its line of half a dozen jewel-like little
lakes. At the end of Tarn Shelf you'll have another choice—instead of heading for the Newdegate Pass you bear right again, this time past Twisted Tarn
and down to Twilight Tarn.

The hut on the corner of Twilight Tarn is a remarkable place. It has been
there more than half a century, and looks as if it has seen better days, but it's
weatherproof enough to be a welcome refuge if the weather turns bad

(which it quickly can). Inside is a variety of rough-hewn furniture and it contains most of the amenities a bushwalker or cross-country skier expects—a fire, a bed and a table. But this hut differs from other walking huts. In one room it houses a substantial collection of old skiing memorabilia. It is not precisely catalogued like a museum collection, but left over the years for the interest of travellers, and viewed and preserved with respect.

The hut was built as a base for cross-country skiing expeditions before the advent of downhill skiing, and still serves that function perfectly well for those who want to use skis for travelling rather than just for rushing downwards.

It looks like the kind of real estate an agent would sell his soul for—perched on the edge of an exquisite little tarn, with a creek running close by, and huddled under the lee of a mountain. But then a real estate agent would probably want to knock down the building and put something a bit more modern there!

Another word of warning about the weather—although the walking is quite easy, at any time of the year the weather can change very suddenly. The shelters along the track are not there for decoration, but for taking refuge from storms. Make sure you and anyone with you carry waterproof clothing, *whatever the weather appears to be doing.*

There are several ways to and from the Twilight Tarn Hut, and a pleasant round trip brings you back to Lake Dobson and your car via Lake Webster and the Fairy Tarn.

How to get there

Twilight Tarn is in Mount Field National Park. Follow the B61 from New Norfolk and take the C609 at the town of National Park. Walking times are advised on an information board at the start of the track.

Narratives from the North

The seizure of Rocky Cape

Rocky Cape in northwestern Tasmania
is a special place. Visible from many miles away
in either direction as you approach on the
highway, it lies on the surface of Bass
Strait like a sleeping dragon.

I ts terrain, its rock, its heath-like vegetation are different from the land nearby. 'A nearer projection, of jagged appearance, was called "Rocky Cape",' wrote Matthew Flinders when he first sighted it in 1798.

Rocky Cape is known to have been the habitat of the Tasmanian Aboriginal people for the last 8000 to 12 000 years—since just after the last Ice Age, in fact. The Tommeginer people lived at 'Tang Dimmer', as they called it, as part of their nomadic range, and their ancestors are thought to have inhabited two particular caves for some 10 000 years.

But from the moment the first white sails came over the horizon, they only had a few thousand days left. In 1827 the settling of Stanley, just along the coast, was the beginning of the end. By 1832 the Aboriginal people of the North-western Tribe were all gone—murdered, driven out or dead from disease.

As recently as 1991 the area was again occupied by the Aboriginal community—this time on similar terms to the way it was taken from them by European settlement. They simply walked in and took it over.

In the middle of the 20th century, there had been considerable interest in this area. Comalco had its eye on the silica mining rights, and fossickers who knew where to look were finding various gemstones, some of them precious. The Burnie Field Naturalists' club had been working for some time to have it preserved as a park. And in 1967, any prospect of the area being mined was put off when 3000 hectares of coastline were proclaimed as Rocky Cape National Park. Since then, 37 shack owners had been allowed to keep non-permanent dwellings there, paying an annual fee to the Circular Head Council and another to the Department of Environment and Planning for an annually renewable licence.

Tasmania's Aboriginal people had for many years been interested in regaining the rights to their tribal lands. After Labor came to power in 1989, it looked as if they would get what they wanted. Land Rights legislation was passed in April 1991 by Tasmania's House of Assembly, granting 53 000 hectares of land to them and making various concessions on ownership, but this Bill was being strongly opposed in the Legislative Council. Rather than just 'hope for the best', the Aboriginal community decided to take action.

'Arrogant, patronising and racist'

On 30 May 1991 a press release announced the seizure of the Rocky Cape National Park by representatives of the Tasmanian Aboriginal community. It said in part:

> ...the Legislative Council have made it clear that the land rights bill before them, which incidentally excludes Rocky Cape, will not be passed. Our patience after 200 years of theft of our lands is wearing thin. The final straw that broke our reliance on the parliamentary process was not so much the likelihood of the Legislative Council blocking the bill, but more so the arrogant, patronising and racist reasons they gave for doing so. We are accustomed to not getting our own way. But we will not be insulted.

On 11 June, 40 Aboriginal people set off in buses from Burnie and set up camp in tents not far from the 37 shacks; in less than a fortnight the camp had swelled to 160 occupants. Two caravans were now set up for families with small children, and the takeover of the park was described as 'an outstanding success'. No police action was taken.

As expected, the Land Rights Bill was defeated in the Upper House on 12 July. Doug Lowe, Labor leader in the Upper House, was very disappointed at the defeat of the Bill, although he did concede that the events at Rocky Cape had done little to help. Michael Mansell declared himself pleased that it was defeated because he thought it was a soft, token bill.

The occupying protesters had put up signs reading 'YOU ARE NOW ON ABORIGINAL LAND'; 'FROM DISPOSSESSION AND OPPRESSION TO REPOSSESSION' and 'THE DISPOSSESSED HAVE REPOSSESSED'. There had previously been signs about the Aboriginal use of the park, but before the occupation they had been the subject of racist vandalism.

Unfortunately this vandalism was reciprocated by some of the Aboriginal community, who apparently broke into shacks and trashed them. (Following these incidents, which shocked the protest organisers, the Tasmanian Aboriginal Centre advertised at the end of November for a substance abuse worker, to be based at Rocky Cape.)

On 1 December, 50 of the protesters moved their camp to a picnic site even closer to the shacks—bringing portable toilets with them so that they could not be accused of breaking the law by camping where no facilities existed. The day after that they issued notices to shack owners in the area:

> As from this day forth, 2nd December 1991, the original owners of the land upon which this house is built have resumed its ownership. All future lease payments are to be paid to the Tasmanian Aboriginal Community. For contractual details contact the Tasmanian Aboriginal Centre, 198 Elizabeth Street, Hobart.

Some saw the move to the picnic site as a deliberate attempt to provoke physical confrontation. The then Premier, Michael Field, saw it as obstruction of normal recreational activities in the park. He called on them to leave the area, and said that he would give them a temporary licence to occupy another site. The move, which was intended to create new interest in the six-month-old protest and focus attention on land rights, had succeeded.

The Government had already withdrawn the park ranger from Rocky Cape, possibly in an attempt to avoid the type of conflict the Aboriginal community appeared to be seeking.

On 6 December the protesters raised the stakes again, by blocking the only road to Rocky Cape with buses. Residents, they said, would have free admittance, but visitors had to pay from two to five dollars and sign permits. People arriving at the blockade were greeted by the sight of spear-sharpening going on at the roadside, though whether this was a cultural or intimidatory statement was not clear. Despite their exemption, the residents were not at all happy about the roadblock. Only one person objected to paying the fee, however; he showed his displeasure by driving into a crowd of protesters, slightly injuring one. (In the end he paid, signed the permit and entered the park.)

Although it looked like an escalation, this blockade signalled the end of the occupation of the site. Mr Field now agreed to meet the protesters and talk to them about land rights in general and Rocky Cape in particular.

This was a change from the careful non-involvement that had gone on before, and the protesters brought to the Devonport meeting a list of agenda items. Mr Field was surprised, he said, that they were so confrontationist towards the Government rather than the Legislative Council—but they were, by this stage, also in conflict with one another. The Tasmanian Aboriginal Land Council (TALC) favoured continuing acts of occupation, while the Tasmanian Aboriginal Centre wanted to work towards land rights by legal methods.

The message of the protest was that they wanted Rocky Cape. In a sense they have achieved this, in that there is now an Aboriginal Steering Committee helping to administer the park. There is also a fairly regular Aboriginal cultural festival at Rocky Cape, featuring traditional crafts, sports (including spear-throwing) and entertainment.

Of more immediate and obvious value to the community was the handing back of a dozen parcels of land in 1995, following a similar occupation at Oyster Cove. These included Oyster Cove, Risdon Cove, South Mount Cameron (or Preminghana), parts of Cape Barren, Babel and Chapel Islands, Badger Island, Big Dog Island, Wybalenna and three cave sites in the World Heritage Area.

A different form of occupation was the Tasmanian Aboriginal Community's purchase of the K-Mart site in Burnie for the record price of $7 million. They are still majority shareholders in this property, and also have interests in Gordon River Cruises and a fish farming enterprise. On a smaller scale, they also own a small shack inside the Rocky Cape National Park (which is still occupied by the TALC).

It will be interesting to trace the future path of Aboriginal Land Rights: will it be physical or fiscal?

How to get there

About 33 kilometres west of Wynyard on the A2, take the C227 for Rocky Cape National Park.

Thanks to Colin Hughes, Tasmanian Aboriginal Land Council, for additional information.

Sisters
Beach

In Tasmania we take it for granted that we
will have easy access to beaches and the sea.
There are resorts and beaches and
agglomerations of holiday homes all around
the State—some of them thriving, others
virtually dormant, and others yet to be developed.
And the 'development' nowadays usually takes
the form of an onslaught by bulldozers,
real estate agents and builders.

Sisters Beach today is a popular and well-known resort—but for over 20 years it was home to just one family, the Irbys. In a scene straight out of the 'Beverly Hillbillies', Mr L.G. Irby, his family and their dog and cat arrived from Hobart in 1933 in an Essex Super 6 touring car groaning under the weight of their possessions, and proceeded to open up the area in true pioneering style.

L.G. Irby, his wife and their four young children cut a 6-kilometre track (for a £44 government bounty) from the Boat Harbour Beach Road to Sisters Beach, and built themselves a bark hut as their first dwelling. The area around was all heath and buttongrass, but L.G. Irby had a theory, which he subsequently proved correct—that with careful application of fertiliser and supplementation of trace elements, pasture and pine trees could be grown here. The thriving gardens and pastures of the present residents show that he was right about this.

The area is still reminiscent of these not-so-early pioneers, as the names show—Irby's Road, Ken's Creek, Bett's Waterfall and Irby Flats. Another secret about the area, and perhaps an even better kept one, is the unique grove of Giant Banksia (*Banksia serrata*) trees. These grow nowhere else in the world except in a couple of small groves on this headland. You drive to the end of the road, by the boat ramp, and from here it's a steep but pleasant walk up from the beach to the track that leads to one of the Banksia groves. The first grove (which unfortunately seems to bear the scars of a recent fire) stands in an extraordinarily peaceful little dip or valley on the hilltop; you can identify the startling Giant Banksia by its long, deeply serrated leaves and its large silvery or golden conical flower heads.

If you continue along the track you will find your way to the mysterious 'wet cave', which looks out over the bay. This sheltered cave is very much larger than its tree-shrouded opening onto the slope would suggest. It is very dark inside, but your eyes gradually become accustomed to the gloom. The cave has apparently never been fully explored—by European settlers at least—but it is thought to extend into the hillside for at least three-quarters of a kilometre, and to contain a reservoir of fresh water up to 10 metres deep! There are stories about its use by escaped convicts (quite possibly true) and about gold coins hidden in its depths (almost certainly untrue).

It is also possible to walk from Sisters Beach through to the Rocky Cape National Park.

How to get there

Off the A2, take the C233 for Sisters Beach,
and drive about 8 kilometres.

'44 kilos of bras please...'

Ever wondered what happens to clothing
or shoes that you take to the Salvation Army?
Or Lifeline? Or the St Vincent
de Paul Society?

I f you've thought about it at all, you probably assumed that you might one day meet someone in the street wearing your jacket or dress or shoes. And you still might. But if the clothing is not suitable for selling in one of the charity shops (often because it's out of date or unfashionably coloured—which doesn't take long nowadays), the only way you'll meet someone wearing it is if you happen to be strolling down the street in Africa or India.

Vincent Industries of Wynyard, a division of the St Vincent de Paul Society, specialises in exporting clothing, footwear and household linen to Africa, and wool and synthetic fibre material to India. This unique exporting enterprise, which started in 1991, sprang out of research which discovered that large quantities of donated material (useless either for welfare or for sale in second-hand shops) were being dumped. This was not a happy state of affairs, not only because of the waste, but because people who donate things to charity expect them to be used. The solution was a bold one—Vincent Industries would take all excess stock from all other charities in Tasmania, sort it, bale it and export it in containers to agents overseas for resale. The profit margins were small, but the combined volume of material was large enough to make it viable.

However, there were problems to be overcome, such as the cost of transhipment (moving containers from one ship to another) in Melbourne—$800 per 6-metre container. This alone was sufficient to make the idea unprofitable. Vincent Industries therefore set up a direct shipping service to Singapore, where transhipment was available at a fraction of this price.

What is sold to the overseas agents is a mixture of used clothing ('2nd and 3rd grade wearables'), footwear, household linen and fibre. Clothes that are too damaged for sale are converted into rags, which are also sold. (So rather than throw something out because you think no-one is likely to wear it, give it to charity. Vincent Industries will find something to do with it.)

Because the export costs are charged by volume, it is important to get as many clothes into the containers as possible. At first, the clothes were put into bales by staff members jumping up and down on them, but now presses do the hard work for them. A 350-tonne double dump press takes this a step further, compressing two bales into the size of one.

One intriguing requirement of the export trade is that everything has to be packed in bales weighing 44 kilograms or less. This is because the agent resells the bales to local traders who carry the bales on their heads and sell them 'door-to-door' until they have earned enough to feed their families and buy another bale!

Another secret about Vincent Industries is that it is mostly staffed by people with disabilities. Although some of the disabled staff have shown great aptitude in sorting fibres (especially wool), others have difficulty with it, so staff without disabilities are employed in some cases. In the area of converting unusable clothing to rags and fibre, however, Vincent Industries has developed its own ultra-safe cutting machine/mutilator, which allows anyone, including staff with physical and mental disabilities, to use the very sharp cutting wheel in safety.

The people who staff the sorting tables also benefit from technology, using an ergonomic sorting table to lift the incoming bales of clothes up to their level so that they don't have to bend over all the time.

Vincent Industries is the only direct exporter of used clothing and fibre in Tasmania, and looks set to expand in the future—especially if our children continue to be so fussy about what's written on their clothes, what diameter their trousers are and exactly how much midriff they do or don't show!

How to get there

You'll find Vincent Industries in Jackson Street, Wynyard, just off Goldie Street, tucked away behind its own thrift shop.

The
mother of
Cradle Mountain-
Lake St Clair
National Park

At Don, near Devonport, in a small
churchyard, stands a gravestone inscribed:
In Loving Memory of Kate Julia
Beloved Wife of Gustav Weindorfer
Died April 29th 1916
Sic Transit Gloria Mundi
Also Gustav Weindorfer
Died May 5th 1932

K ate Weindorfer's lonely grave (which is many kilometres
from her husband's, although the inscription above seems
to suggest that they are both here) is a sad and ironic
reflection of the last years of her life as the wife of Gustav Weindorfer. For
although they loved each other dearly, circumstances forced them to spend
a lot more time a lot further apart than either would have wanted.

Kate Weindorfer (née Cowles) was born in 1863 in Fingal to a former schoolteacher and a wealthy farmer. Her father, an ironmonger by trade, had been a gold miner in his youth, and he knew exactly who made the money on the goldfields. So during the mining boom in the middle of the 19th century he opened a general store at Branxholm, and carted provisions into the mining areas and tin out of them.

By the time Kate's father died in 1894, he had succeeded in several businesses; he not only owned a farm called 'Lauriston', at Kindred, but he had substantial holdings in what was to become the central business district of Devonport.

In his will Kate received an annual allowance of £50 a year, and then when his real estate interests in Devonport were sold seven years later she became completely her own woman. She was now 38 years old and secure for life.

Kate subsequently moved to Melbourne and (having a keen interest in botany) joined the Field Naturalists' Club of Victoria in 1902. It was in this club, because of her botanical expertise, that she met the 27-year-old Austrian immigrant Gustav Weindorfer—who, at the time, was disillusioned with life in Australia and thinking of going home to his native mountains. Kate, unlike many women of her time, was not only financially independent, but an independent thinker as well. She had already contributed papers to the *Victorian Naturalist*, among them one on Mount Roland in Tasmania. She and Weindorfer immediately hit it off and became fast friends. They were both keen on botany and music—she could play three instruments, and he had a good singing voice—and not surprisingly, he now decided to stay in Australia.

In 1905 they became engaged to be married. After careful scrutiny of 'Dorfer' (as Gustav was better known) by her family (and after he became a British citizen) they were married in 1906 in Tasmania, in her brother's house at Stowport—a second choice, the first venue having burned down!

The pair then set off on a five-week camping honeymoon on Mount Roland. This was significant for two reasons—first, for the series of tongue-in-cheek stories they wrote for the local newspapers; and second, for the fact that it was from here that Gustav Weindorfer first spotted Cradle Mountain.

They then took up married life in earnest, with Gustav initially working for Kate's brother Dan, and then the pair of them setting up their own 50-hectare farm at Kindred. Kate had persuaded Dan to sell her this piece of land from the family property, 'Lauriston'. They built a cottage on it and called it 'Roland Lea'. Both were hard workers, and Gustav was by profession an estate manager, so Kate's farm was to generate a handy income for them in the years to come.

Their interest in the bush and botany continued, and in 1909 they climbed Cradle Mountain (in the snow) for the first time—Kate being the first European woman to climb it. It was here that Gustav uttered his famous declaration:

> This must be a national park for the people for all time. It is magnificent, and people must know about it and enjoy it.

Logging was a major worry to them and to their plans for the area, so in 1910 they took an unusual approach to conservation. They and several friends bought adjoining 100-hectare parcels of land at Cradle Mountain.

On the newly acquired land they then began to build a chalet in the Austrian style, calling it *Waldheim*—'forest home'. Interestingly enough, although 'Waldheim' has always been identified with Weindorfer himself, it was actually built on Kate's land, not his.

This venture was even more far-sighted than it appears. Not only was it an early and successful foray into conservation, it was also one of the first wilderness tourism developments in Tasmania. It was always intended that the chalet would be open to paying tourists, who could stay in it, eat in it and be guided on bushwalking, skiing, hunting and mountaineering tours.

After they finished 'Waldheim' in 1912 they had to run two homes. For the most part, Kate ran 'Roland Lea' and Gustav the chalet. When she could, Kate came out to Cradle Mountain to help Gustav look after the visitors, and when he could get away he would help on the farm; but both found the long separations hard.

Although they leased 'Roland Lea' and attempted to live full-time at the now-profitable 'Waldheim', 1914 was a year that was destined to go badly for the Weindorfers. Not only was England suddenly at war with Germany, but Kate fell ill. The diagnoses included heart disease, lung problems and indigestion. But it went deeper than any of these. She was only able to spend four months at 'Waldheim' before health problems forced her to go back out to Kindred. If they had found separation hard before, it was even worse now. On one day Gustav made three trips to Ulverstone to see her in hospital.

It seems quite likely that Kate had breast cancer—there was a lump in her breast, which was X-rayed. Certainly her decline through weakness, debility and pain over the next year or so had much in common with cancer, although the eventual cause of death (at the age of 52) was shown as 'acute nephritis and uraemia' (kidney disease).

Weindorfer missed her dreadfully—all the more so because he had a difficult time after her death. World War I was now in full and terrible swing, and local gossip had him spying and working behind the lines for the Germans. The antipathy, unfortunately, was not confined to the general public—Kate's own family felt that the rigours of life at 'Waldheim' had hastened her death.

Weindorfer still had a lot of friends, but he had lost the friend he valued most. However, she had not abandoned him. Kate had altered her will to make sure that after her death Gustav would own both 'Waldheim' and 'Roland Lea'.

In life she had given him help, support, encouragement and good ideas throughout their short time together. In death, she now gave him financial independence when he needed it, and ensured that he would be able to concentrate his energies on their project—which was to become the Cradle Mountain–Lake St Clair National Park.

It is quite likely that had he not met Kate Cowles, Weindorfer would have gone back to Austria. There is certainly no reason to suppose he would have come to Tasmania. Even if he had, could he have afforded to buy 100 hectares of land at Cradle Mountain?

If Gustav is the father of the Cradle Mountain–Lake St Clair National Park, then Kate is its mother. And yet, because of her early death, there are people who have no idea that she existed, let alone where she is buried.

How to get there

The little cemetery where Kate is buried is in Stony Rise Road
at Don, a few hundred metres up the road from the Don River Railway Museum.
Gustav is buried in the Cradle Mountain–Lake St Clair National Park,
which is easy enough to find.

Dorfer's
death

Although Gustav Weindorfer, the man, is
well-known, the manner of his death is not.
(Motorcyclists in particular will sympathise.)

H is main mode of transport was an Indian motorcycle
and sidecar he had bought in 1931, and he used it for
coming and going between 'Waldheim' and his farm
at Ulverstone. In May 1932, preparing to leave 'Waldheim' and spend the
winter in Launceston, he was having some difficulty with the motorcycle.
He wrote to a friend:

> Here I am writing after three days trying to kick some life into my
> motor bike—and at last it went this morning only to stop whenev-
> er I put the thing into low gear. Probably magneto trouble and moist
> air. I hope to make her go tomorrow and am off down to the coast.

He did not make her go tomorrow, and he never reached the coast. A
friend found his body the next day nearly a kilometre from the chalet. He
was lying beside the motorcycle, apparently in the act of kick-starting it.

It appeared that he had run the bike down the hill from 'Waldheim', trying without success to bump-start it, and when it stopped in a hollow
he had then set up a block and tackle to get it up the next hill. As the
sidecar outfit was no lightweight, and as he was not young, the effort of
continuing to try to start it caused him to have a fatal heart attack. He had
a history of heart trouble, but apparently he made no concessions to it.

On hearing of his death, Fred Smithies and several friends determined
that he should be buried at 'Waldheim', and got permission to take his body
back in from Sheffield. To do this they had to tramp 12 kilometres in rain
from their car, carry the coffin along a twisty, slippery track, and then dig
the grave themselves. He was buried on 10 May 1932 at his 'forest home'.

G.J. Coles

On the main (and just about the only)
street in Wilmot, there is an old store, which
looks entirely in character with the old town.
What makes this store unique is the
name above it—G.J. Coles.

This is the first Coles store in Australia, the prototype for your local supermarket. Amazingly, it is
still pretty much the same as it used to be, and it
has the look of having been left that way rather than 'dressed up'. An
incredible mish-mash of goods can be bought here, and old toys and uten-
sils fill every corner. This is a store that knows what it is, but it is no
Disneyland experience. Just real charm, from the dusty boards underfoot to
the high and slightly tatty ceilings.

The house next door is the original Coles home, and very grand it is.
Tasmania is lucky to have both buildings—and lucky, too, that they are out
in Wilmot rather than in the path of a property developer wanting to build
yuppie batteries in Hobart or Launceston.

How to get there

Wilmot isn't really on the way to or from anywhere. You have
to want to get there. However, the drive is rewarding, whichever way
you go. The easiest way to describe it (so that you can find it on the
map and work out a route) is that it's on the C132, directly south
of Ulverstone and about 25 kilometres away as the crow flies. The last
time we went there, we did a trip that took us south to Cethana
and from there to Tasmazia and Sheffield.

The amazing
mazes
of Tasmazia

The ancient word 'maze' means to daze
or stupefy. 'Amazing' comes from it. The world's
first, most famous and supposedly most difficult
maze is said to have been the labyrinth of King
Minos of Crete, a huge network of tunnels
in which lived the Minotaur.

H alf-man, half-bull, he gave a certain spice to getting
lost in the Labyrinth until he met Theseus, who
cheated on him with a ball of string and then cheated on the lady who gave him the string.

But where is the largest maze in the world? Disneyland? Hampton
Court? Somewhere in Europe? No (allegedly, at least), it's near Promised
Land, between Sheffield and Lake Barrington in Tasmania.

Tasmazia, 'the world's largest maze complex', is so far off the beaten track
that it's hard to imagine what possessed its owner to set up here. However,
the tourist buses do come and their cargoes dutifully wander around getting lost in the half-dozen mazes. There are a couple of novelty mazes (for
kids and claustrophobics), but in terms of true 'get-lost' masses of obstruc-
tions, there are five: the Great Maze (the world's largest), the Hampton

Court Maze (which is an exact copy of the famous Hampton Court maze), the Hexagonal Maze, the Confusion Maze and the Cage. This last, says the literature, is 'not for the faint-hearted', but we didn't find it too worrisome. It is a bit more closed in than the hedge mazes, however.

Is it the world's largest maze and maze complex? The competition is formidable. Official figures show the Longleat Maze at Longleat House in England as the longest hedge maze in terms of path length (2.72 kilometres), while the Marlborough Maze at Blenheim Palace, also in England, is the largest symbolic hedge maze. The largest in area is the 8740-square metre hedge maze at Ruurlo in the Netherlands. However, the most recent of these figures is from 1995, while the Tasmazia hedges were still growing. An application from Tasmazia is with the Guinness Book of World Records at the time of writing, so time will tell. Not that these figures matter much. When you're lost in the middle of a seemingly never-ending tunnel of greenery, it is no consolation to know that you are somewhere inside the world's largest maze. Quite the reverse!

The owners/growers/builders/mazers of the complex and its attached pancake parlour are Brian and Laura Inder, who have been planting and tending their mazes since 1988. They are escapees from a successful life in the corporate rat-race, and have succeeded in getting about as far away from it all as is possible to get.

How to get there

We won't give you detailed instructions for how
to get there. If you can't find a maze complex by yourself,
it's hardly fair to direct you to one. (But here's
a clue—it's on the C140.)

Yes, there is a Sawdust Bridge

Not far from Kate Weindorfer's grave there is a bridge rejoicing in the name of 'The Sawdust Bridge'. This narrow little footbridge spans the Don River near the swimming pool and almost meets the Don River Railway.

There are probably gullible tourists being told right now that the bridge is built from compacted sawdust held together with bullock dung, but the truth is far less picturesque and infinitely more practical.

The Sawdust Bridge, built from bush timber, was the first bridge over any of the northwest rivers and was built by the River Don Trading Company. Originally called the Tramway Bridge (for reasons lost to memory, although perhaps it was meant to link up with a tramway), it was designed to carry foot traffic—both human and horse. It got its name from the fact that on the western side there was a sawmill which produced vast heaps of sawdust and spewed them out along the bank.

The pathway through these provided a meandering but dry approach to the bridge.

Unfortunately, frequent floods meant that the bridge was constantly being damaged and in need of repair. Because it was a privately owned bridge it was not seen as the responsibility of the council, so various working bees and community occasions were held to keep it in repair. At the end of the 19th century it was completely destroyed in a flood and rebuilt. It has gone through a succession of repairs since then (some with council help) and in 1988 was finally reconstructed to its present state as part of the Australian Bicentenary celebrations.

How to get there

Drive down past the Don River Railway Museum to the Don River. Cross the river and turn right into Waverley Road. Follow the road for about a kilometre until you see the bridge.

Big man, big heart

If you are driving through Tarleton,
and you happen to see a 3.5-metre high
cartoon of a gigantic axeman, then you have
found the home of David Foster,
woodchopper extraordinaire.

Winner of more World Championships than any axeman in history, David Foster has been competing and winning since 1975. It's safe to say that if he is in the ring, the other axemen are competing for second place—unless it's a handicap event, in which case he is still a threat even when he gives away half a minute to the front markers!

Tasmania is probably the world capital of woodchopping, the sport where the object is simply to sever your log faster than anyone else. Sometimes you're standing beside it (the standing log); sometimes you're standing on it (underhand); sometimes you're wielding a saw; and sometimes you climb up a tree and sever the top (treefelling—the one area in which David does not compete). Woodchopping is explosive, violent and exciting to watch. The axes are so sharp that you could shave with them if you were brave enough, and they are wielded at terrifying speed by seriously BIG men.

And David Foster is probably the biggest. He is immense—some two metres tall and weighing about 190 kilograms—so it's not surprising that when he hits a log, the ground shakes and the axe cuts deep. What is surprising is how fast he hits (faster than anyone else) and how fast he moves. But don't take our word for it. Go to any country show where woodchopping is featured and you're likely to see him in action. You'll also find him friendly and approachable when he isn't actually swinging an axe or focusing on the next chop.

The sport in which he is such an unassailable champion is still a bit of a secret, thanks to amateurish and haphazard promotion; and he himself is perhaps best known for his Tooheys beer commercials with David Boon. But there is a side to David Foster that is an even better kept secret—which is how readily he makes himself available to charities for promotional work. If an organisation is trying to help the battlers, make things easier for disadvantaged kids, or just bring a little sunshine into dark lives, they know that David Foster will help if he can. He has in the past driven on the same day from one end of the State to the other, at his own expense, so that he can squeeze in more than one charity event. And he doesn't just stand there. He gets in and has a go. Whether there is money to be collected, garbage to be picked up, or entertainment to be provided, David will be in the thick of it.

Of course, he isn't perfect. He's been known to utter the odd expletive. His sense of humour gets him in trouble occasionally. He's not keen on coming second (though he accepts it graciously on the rare occasions when he is beaten). He's expensive to feed.

When the chips are down—or in his case, flying through the air in vast lumps—there is no finer axeman in the world. And yet he's a man who is proud of his roots in Tasmania and totally in touch with reality. He is also proud of what he can do, and works hard to make sure he can keep doing it.

In his book, *The Power of Two: The David Foster Story* (a good read provided you can stomach his other weakness—puns) David invites you to honk your horn if you're passing, or, if he's in the garden, to yell out a greeting or stop and have a yarn. Try that at any other multiple world champion's house and you may be eaten by Rottweilers.

How to get there

Tarleton is on the B19 between Spreyton and Latrobe.

Bakers
Beach

Bakers Beach, on the east side of
Port Sorell, is today part of the Narawntapu
National Park. It used to be called the
Asbestos Range National Park, after the
asbestos (not to mention copper, iron and gold)
that was mined here, but this name was
thought to be politically incorrect.

T his national park is not one of Tasmania's 'name' parks
like Cradle Mountain–Lake St Clair or Freycinet, but
it has a charm of its own. We arrived there in the late
afternoon, and when we stepped out of the dunes and onto the long, long
curve of the beach we were the only people on it.

It's hard to imagine Bakers Beach having anything to do with Lake
Eyre—apart from the amount of salt in the air—but they are related in
being the two places where consecutive Australian Land Speed Records
were set in the 1960s. The Lake Eyre effort has passed into history (as it
was also the World Land Speed Record, set by the late Sir Donald
Campbell at 644 kilometres per hour); but the previous record, set in
1961 on Bakers Beach, has faded from all but a few memories.

The idea of breaking the Australian Land Speed Record was that of Austin ('Aussie') Miller of Launceston, who had recently imported a Cooper Formula One racing car to Tasmania from England. It was quite a fast car, with a Coventry-Climax racing engine, but Aussie had another engine in mind for it—a 4.7-litre Chevrolet Corvette V-8 engine from a racing boat. The record was then held by Ted Gray in his 'Tornado' at 157.5 miles per hour (252 kilometres per hour).

Aussie's mechanic Geoff Smedley installed the monstrous engine in the little car, built a 2-speed gearbox for it and created a perspex cowling to cover the driver's head, and they set off for the 7-kilometre expanse of Bakers Beach, which was already in regular use as a racing track for cars and motorcycles.

On the morning of 20 November 1961, Aussie and his crew rolled the little yellow car out onto the sand and prepared to make history. Unfortunately they discovered that the timing wire was about 275 metres short of the 'mile'—land speed records being measured then over a flying mile (1.609 kilometres). Fortunately the local police were on hand. They radioed Devonport police station to organise some more wire, and a car was sent out to meet the 'courier.'

While they waited, Aussie and his crew decided to attack the flying quarter-mile record, for which they did have enough wire. The speed was to be calculated as the average of one run in each direction (to allow for the wind) and Aussie's first run was over 150 miles per hour (270 kilometres per hour). On the return run, however, the perspex canopy cracked, came off, and ripped off the engine cover as well, so that he finished his run exposed to the blast of a 270-kilometres per hour wind, with the canopy and cowling dragging on the sand behind the car.

When the extra wire arrived from Devonport, Aussie climbed back in the car (this time with neither windscreen nor perspex bubble) and fired up the engine again. On the longer course, the car was able to get closer to its theoretical maximum—it was geared for 320 kilometres per hour—and his first run took him through the mile in just over 13 seconds for 172 miles per hour or 275 kilometres per hour. The return run into a strong headwind was slower, but it was still good enough for an average speed of 164 miles per hour (262 kilometres per hour)—which was a new Australian Record, comfortably faster than the old one. It took Campbell's million-dollar Bluebird to beat it, and in fact, had Aussie Miller been on Lake Eyre he could probably have gone a lot faster. The car was fishtailing in the damp sand, and he kept it to 6000 rpm instead of letting it go to its maximum engine speed of 7000 rpm.

Just over the dunes from the beach (which, you may be relieved to hear, is no longer used for motor racing) is a network of campgrounds and picnic shelters—no different, on the face of it, from any other national park.

What makes this national park special is that it is a wildlife, and particularly wombat, metropolis. Animal watching is best done at dusk, but at any time of day you can usually see a good selection of wallabies, pademelons and big forester kangaroos. And there are birds of every species, from waders to cockatoos to sea eagles.

At dusk, it's a night on the town for the local wildlife. They appear from everywhere to enjoy the rich grazing that was created when this area was cleared for farmland by the same Mr Baker who gave the beach its name.

You might think there are no wombats (although if you've walked even a short distance in daylight you will have seen virtually streets of their palatial burrows); but then you notice that what looks like a rock is now in a different place. You walk purposefully towards it and it shambles away. If you're ham-footed enough it may even run away. But if you approach carefully you can come quite close to one of these endearing, bear-like animals. And when you turn to leave its company you'll notice that there are others—lots of them. In fact, if you want to be guaranteed that you will see a wombat, Bakers Beach is the place to go.

Wombats have a character similar to Mr Badger in *The Wind in the Willows*—strong, determined, yet shy of 'company'. In fact they are commonly known to country Tasmanians as badgers.

It would be tempting, then, to imagine that Badger Beach, Badger Head and Little Badger Head just up the coast are named after the proliferation of wombats in the area—but they're not.

At the start of the 19th century, a young convict woman named Charlotte Badger jumped overboard from a ship moored off the coast, and was taken in by the local Aboriginal people at the headland called Norroundboo. She remained at large, and in fact was seen in Tonga in 1816 (small world, even then) with a child in tow. Obviously a resourceful young woman, and a loss to the new colony—even if her overseers wouldn't have seen it that way!

How to get there

Nineteen kilometres west of Frankford on the B71, near the Franklin Rivulet, is the turn-off (C740) for Narawntapu National Park. Bakers Beach is 17 kilometres down this road.

The
dredge
and the
cruiser

Internet users today are known to get
impatient if they have to wait more than
10 seconds for something to happen; shoppers
get very testy after 10 minutes. At the turn of the
century the Launceston Marine Board had to
wait 10 *years* for an order to be fulfilled.

I f you stand anywhere on the banks of the Tamar River and watch the big ships come in, you may wonder how it is that the channel is deep enough to accommodate them. The answer any of the locals will give you is 'Ponrabbel'. That's a Tasmanian Aboriginal word describing the whole area; but it's also the name given to a little dredge that (in various incarnations) gave a new meaning to the words 'chequered career'.

By the end of the 19th century the Launceston Marine Board had a large number of vessels in the water all the time, dredging a passage up the river to Launceston. It was usually possible for ships up to 3000–4000 tonnes to use the channel. Unfortunately, however, the silt from the banks had a habit of filling it up again.

The Launceston Marine Board had already commissioned a new dredge from the Scottish shipyards that was up to the task of keeping the channel clear, but unfortunately it had proved not to be up to the task of getting to Tasmania. It had sunk in a storm on the way out.

In 1913, another dredge, the *Ponrabbel*, was ordered from Ferguson Brothers of the Clyde, and in May 1914 she set sail (literally—she had been fitted with a taller mast so that she could sail as a ketch) for Tasmania under Captain Rogers.

Rogers (who had insisted on wages being paid in advance for himself and the crew in case she followed her sister ship to the bottom) had only got as far as Wales when he began to have doubts about the wisdom of the voyage and the dredge's suitability for it. Having paid out for the previous dredge, the *Ponrabbel*'s insurers were insisting that she sail down the coast of Africa and around the Cape of Good Hope instead of taking the short route across the Mediterranean and through the Suez Canal. The rough waters of the Irish Sea were enough to convince Rogers that this was not a good idea, although the reason for it was sound enough—the insurers wanted to avoid the monsoon season, and reasoned that taking the long way around would do it. They were, however, prepared to cover the boat against loss from enemy action. World War I was under way, but evidently they deemed this loss unlikely.

Eventually the insurers agreed to let her go through the Suez Canal if she waited until after the monsoon was over. This she did, under a new captain; but in October, five months after setting out, she met the German light cruiser *Emden* southeast of Sri Lanka, off the Maldives.

The *Emden* was fast becoming a legend in the Indian Ocean. Operating with no base, and refuelling and provisioning from the ships she captured or sank, she came and went as she pleased—despite being pursued by over 70 British ships. In her short life she sank some 20 ships, and Captain von Muller and his crew were already known for their chivalry and courtesy towards their captives.

Emden was in the throes of taking prizes from another ship when the *Ponrabbel* was sighted on the horizon, and because of her unusual profile she was taken for an enemy torpedo boat—a serious threat to the *Emden*. Just as the decks were about to be cleared for action, someone spotted the mistake and identified her as a seagoing dredge—no threat to a cruiser at all. *Emden*'s crew fell about with laughter and hailed *Ponrabbel*. When they boarded her, her captain and crew were already lined up on deck, packed and ready to leave. They had been paid for their voyage, they explained, and so were glad to be off her; and *Emden*'s reputation was well-known.

The *Emden* duly sank the *Ponrabbel*—which thereby gained the dubious distinction of being one of the first ships sunk in the war—and put the crew ashore unharmed in India. (*Emden* herself had not long to live; she was sunk by HMAS *Sydney* less than a month later.)

The insurance payout was sufficient for yet another *Ponrabbel* to be built, but she was not completed until 1920 because of the war. Captain Smith and his crew must have had considerable forebodings, given the fate of her two predecessors and the fact that she had no radio; and their fears were realised when she developed steering problems off the Portuguese coast and had to divert to Lisbon. Unfortunately she ran aground in fog 80 kilometres out, and remained aground for 11 days until towed off by another ship.

After repairs and rudder modifications in Gibraltar she continued her journey. She had now been en route for some five months, and had an almost entirely new crew and a new skipper, Captain Manning—the original crew having gratefully gone home.

Even before she left the Mediterranean she was in trouble again, nearly sinking in heavy seas and springing enough leaks to take in over 600 millimetres of water a day. In Malta she had to have an additional bilge pump and repairs to her plating. Extra caulking was needed in Aden, and by the time she reached Singapore she had just about had another change of crew due to sickness and infections.

When she arrived at George Town in April 1921, she had been at sea for 8 months, with only 87 days spent steaming. Captain Manning obviously believed that it's an ill wind that blows nobody good, since he remained in Tasmania for some time giving lectures on his epic voyage.

When she took up her duties in the Tamar after such a shaky start, it could hardly have been expected that *Ponrabbel* would last long. But she stayed at work for the next 56 years, dredging up several million tonnes of river bottom, straightening the channel where necessary and finally making it some 10 metres deeper than it had been at the turn of the century. Her clattering and banging became a familiar sound to anyone who lived along the Tamar—especially when she was involved in shaping Garden Island as it is today.

She even made her own little bits of history—discovering the wreck of HMS *Porpoise*, for example, while clearing away the rock that had sunk the vessel over 150 years before.

When *Ponrabbel* was finally dismantled in 1977, a piece of maritime history left the Tamar River. But at least it was a deeper Tamar.

Low Head

Many thousands of people pass
through George Town every year and it's
a safe bet that many of them know very
little about the real extent
of the town.

T hey may visit the town centre, or they may
notice, if they are out on the river, that the town
extends for a considerable distance towards the
mouth of the Tamar. But unless they have a particular reason for doing so,
most will never bother to look at Low Head, 6 kilometres north of
George Town.

Tourism is not exactly encouraged by the old Launceston families who
have their holiday homes on Low Head. No doubt the families built here
for peace and quiet and want to keep it that way. However, there is nothing to stop you driving out to see Low Head.

One local resident who took peace and quiet to extremes was Fred
Gunn of the Launceston timber family, who early in the 20th century built
a stone castle in the grounds of his holiday home, 'Kuranui', so that he
could 'get away from the children'. He called it 'Castle Thurso', after the
Scottish port from which the first Gunn, Alexander, had sailed for Tasmania
100 years before. It was built from local stone, with the more readily work-
able bluestone being brought in from Launceston for the corners of the

walls. It looks like a miniature medieval castle, complete with tower, battlements and arched doorway; but you'll need sharp eyes to spot it, as it's almost completely hidden by trees.

Not far from the end of the Low Head Road you'll see the group of buildings that constitutes the Pilot Station. One or more pilots have been on duty at the mouth of the Tamar since 1804. The Pilot Station was unusual (from the 1830s on, at least) in being so close to a lighthouse, and the pilots have had a long and close relationship with the lighthouse and its keepers. As the lighthouse keeper was likely to be the first to see ships headed for the Tamar, it became traditional for the keeper to dip the flag to let the pilots know they were required.

It was also possible for people in Launceston to know about the arrival of ships within minutes, since a semaphore system was set up from Low Head to Mount George to Mount Direction and finally to Windmill Hill in Launceston. (After the invention of the telegraph, people were heard to complain that it sometimes wasn't as quick as the old system.) The semaphore stations are being restored and should be back in action by the time you read this.

Other occupants of Low Head are the fairy penguins, who nest and raise their young in burrows in the flat land that leads down to the sea between the Pilot Station and the lighthouse. The chicks stay in the burrows, while the parents go out to sea fishing. Every night they return after dark to feed the chicks. You can see them all year round, provided you are prepared to wait quietly and watch in the dark. There is a viewing platform near the water, and a local company runs nocturnal tours.

At the end of the road, of course, is the Low Head lighthouse, first built in 1833 and only the third lighthouse built in Australia. (It is also Tasmania's most accessible lighthouse.) A light at this point was viewed as an absolute necessity because of the dangers of Bass Strait, the reefs at the mouth of the Tamar and the difficulty of getting up and down the river at any time. Hebe Reef alone, just outside the mouth, accounted for the loss of many vessels—and continued to do so even after the lighthouse was built. The original was not well built, and had to be replaced 55 years later by a man rejoicing in the name of 'Bolting Dick' Warmsley!

Various updates to the lights have taken place since the row of small kerosene lamps that first formed the lantern. The candlepower has grown ever greater, kerosene has (since 1937) been replaced by electricity; even the keeper has now been replaced by a computerised system.

The 15-metre lighthouse still standing is the same one that was built in 1888, and acquired its distinctive red band in 1926 to help aircraft pick it out easily. A foghorn was also added in 1929. Its three-blast-per-minute pattern could be heard from nearly 10 kilometres out to sea, and from Port Sorell, Bellingham or Exeter on land. Local residents say that at first it made sleeping difficult on foggy nights, but later became just one of the reassuring sounds of home. It ceased operation in 1973. (The foghorn itself is still there, and at time of writing is under restoration.)

It was from East Beach, 'behind' Low Head, that the first undersea telegraph cable was laid between Tasmania and Victoria. Although messages were successfully sent, the cable's outer sheath wasn't up to the punishment from Bass Strait and the project was abandoned in 1861 after numerous breakdowns.

Eight years later a private company succeeded where the government had failed, and the first Tasmania-to-England telegram was sent as early as 1872. This cable occasionally parted too, but it was always easily fixed. Twelve years later a second cable was laid parallel to the first, as a contingency measure.

Although the Bass Strait cable no longer runs from East Beach, the headquarters of the cable company still stands, between the Pilot Station and the penguin colony. It was at one time a holiday home for nuns, but is now a private holiday home. Another sign of the company's presence is the position of the creek that empties onto East Beach. It originally came out at the western end of the beach, but they were worried about it interfering with the cable and diverted it to flow into the sea at the other end. Needless to say, it's slowly making its way back down the beach to its original home.

The Gunn family had also been active with stone in the 1880s, building a large fish trap at the western end of East Beach. This was 'restored' by Jack Curtis, and in the 1960s it became a tradition among the kids in the area to go with Mr Curtis to empty the trap and get some free fish for the family. Sadly, it's no longer there.

How to get there

When you enter George Town on the main (A8) road, you will come to a roundabout. Instead of going left down Macquarie Street, go straight on, on the Low Head Road.

Wilderness
in the
city

Where else in Australia, or any other
country, could you find 170 hectares of bushland
teeming with wild animals, just one kilometre
from the centre of a city? In Launceston's
Cataract Gorge, you can see exactly that.

T he Gorge, with its unlimited supply of fresh water
from the South Esk River, was a major reason for
the choice of Launceston (rather than George
Town) as the main settlement in the north.

The Gorge extends west from the King's Bridge, and is used for everything from picnicking to nature rambles, from swimming to rock climbing.
A book has been written on the Gorge's rock climbs, which are unique in
the level of interaction they allow between climbers and spectators!

Of Tasmania's 35 species of native mammals, 16 can be seen in the
Gorge. You will also find some 300 major plant species, 10 different rep-
tiles and a couple of frogs. The river has every type of fish you could wish
for, and as recently as the 1990s it hosted both an elephant seal and a fur
seal! The air is even richer, with over 50 bird species—three of them (the
swift parrot, the peregrine falcon and the Australian owlet-nightjar) of

conservation significance because of increasing rarity. If it's rare to find this much wildlife this close to the city, how much rarer is it to find endangered wildlife in such close company with its biggest threat—human beings! Peacocks are not native, but you can see them wandering through the grounds of the First Basin, evidently in harmony with the natives.

The plants, the birds and the animals do not exist here in isolation—they share their habitat with some half a million visitors annually. And this sharing has been going on since the first settlement. Launceston people have always wanted the Gorge to be the way it is, and have usually resisted change unless it was to the obvious benefit of the Gorge or the people of the city.

A proposal to dam the Gorge was opposed on aesthetic grounds in 1844—a time when aesthetic and environmental concerns were not as fashionable as they are now. Yet the water has been used. It powered the original Ritchie's Mill, and parts of the weir and flume that carried the water can still be seen where the First Basin joins the Cataract. Further down it was used to wash clothes, and had its own professional 'washerman'. The water was also sold (upstream, one hopes) for drinking water.

The City and Suburbs Improvement Organisation began serious development of the Gorge in 1890, with the construction of the footpath to the First Basin. The gatehouse, where the threepenny toll for using the path was paid, still stands at the Kings Bridge.

The South Esk has always been used for swimming, and from 1895 onwards it powered the Duck Reach Power Station. Duck Reach was the largest 19th-century electric power generation installation in Australia, the largest hydroelectric scheme of its time and the first major supplier to any city in Australia.

While there is nothing secret about an environment that 500 000 people visit every year, what is remarkable is how little impact they continue to have on it; the Cataract Gorge demonstrates that we can exist alongside and very close to nature, if we really want to.

How to get there

Paterson Street leads to the Kings Bridge, which is at one end of the Gorge. If you cross the Bridge and keep on going up Trevallyn Road, this becomes Gorge Road and will eventually take you through the gates that lead to the Tea Rooms car park at the First Basin.

Gourlays

Remember lolly shops?
Remember the wonderful glass
jars full of delights such as Aniseed Bon
Bons, Acid Drops, Humbugs and Bullseyes?
If we saw their like today we'd view them as
a cornucopia of hyperactivity and whisk
the kids away quickly before they
saw them. Or would we?

There is a genuine old-fashioned lolly shop, so old-fashioned that it probably thinks of itself as a sweet shop, in Launceston's Quadrant Mall. It is called Gourlays, and it's been in the business of making fine confectionery for over 100 years. They still believe in hand-making everything and still display their stock in hand-labelled jars (although nowadays they're plastic).

Not everything in the shop is made by Gourlays, but among the row upon row of confectionery it's easy to spot their own produce, because the jars are all colour-coded. Every jar has a Gourlays label, and the ones they make themselves have a brown border. Blue lids are for liquorice, and there is a considerable amount of the Dutch salted variety.

Apart from the vast assortment of boiled lollies, you can also buy many different flavours of fudge, traditional toffee, lollipops, handmade chocolates (special boxes of which are made for Mother's Day) and an assortment of other oddities.

One of the oddities is their joint top seller (with Acid Drops), the Snowball—a marshmallow covered with chocolate and coconut. Others are Coconut Roughs, Jockey Caps (or Esmereldas), Tassie Rock (like the Blackpool variety) and Strawberry Krokettes (strawberry marshmallow covered in chocolate).

The factory (which seems a vulgar name—maybe it should be 'manufactory') is at the Penny Royal Complex; and unlike the flour windmill it actually does what it appears to be doing. You can watch the sweets/lollies being made too—except in August, when it closes for cleaning, maintenance and staff holidays.

So if you fancy eating something that will instantly transport you back to your childhood and doesn't feel like it could equally well be called chemical mouthwash, take a trip to the Quadrant Mall and try some of Gourlays' confections.

The Old Umbrella Shop

Launceston's No. 60 George Street, whose windows declare it to be the premises of 'R. Shott & Son', has been described as the last genuine early Victorian shop in Tasmania.

T oday it belongs to the National Trust, and apart from the proliferation of National Trust-related items on sale it looks exactly as it did when Mr Shott, the umbrella maker, moved in (from next door) in 1921. The shop is still lined with blackwood and full of umbrellas. The umbrellas and walking sticks Mr Shott originally sold were made from whalebone (specifically, sperm whale jawbone), often inlaid with mother of pearl or ivory, and many are on display in the shop.

You can still buy umbrellas and walking sticks in the shop—in fact, according to the volunteers who work here, the modern ones sell very well—but its principal purpose is just being there, acting as a gift shop and information centre and representing the National Trust.

Walking into it is like walking back 100 years—even the telephone is a large black bakelite one—and the trip, through both space and time, is worth making. You may also want to buy an umbrella. And it's certainly the place to go for that.

The **Pirate** Pickwick

It is ironic that one of the most
sought-after collectors' books ever to
come out of Tasmania is also one that was
almost certainly illegally published. When
Charles Dickens' *Pickwick Papers* was first
published in Britain in 1836, it came out in
a series of 20 episodes. It was a publishing
phenomenon, selling tens of thousands
of copies of each issue as soon as
they came off the presses.

Copyright laws were evidently not as rigidly enforced back then as they are today, because a printer named Henry Dowling of Launceston immediately set to work to produce his own edition. (He apparently trusted that Tasmania was too far away for Dickens' lawyers to worry about him.)

Like the original publishers, he brought his edition out in 20 parts, and followed these with a collected edition. The collected edition itself was on sale within two years of the original, so Mr Dowling didn't waste any time getting it out.

In his preface Dowling writes (among other puffery) of his hope that:

> …it will be pronounced by the public to be the best executed typo-graphical work that has been published in these Colonies. The publisher can assure his subscribers that no trouble or expense has been spared to secure it such a distinction.

One expense he does appear to have avoided is getting the permission of Mr Dickens or his publishers. As one commentator points out, he was such an excellent self-publicist that if he could have used Dickens' imprimatur then he certainly would have!

He even commissioned new illustrations, which he describes as 'fully equal to the original'. That they are fully equal is not surprising, as they are copies. Another expense he seems to have spared himself is that of getting copies made of half the illustrations. His book has 20, while the original has over 40. Even the unknown artist entered into the piratical spirit of the enterprise. As the original artist was called 'Phiz,' he has signed himself 'Tiz'—except where he has just written 'Phiz.'

The book sold enormously well all over Australia; and it is precisely because it was so popular that it has become so rare. Everyone wanted to read it and the books, good though they were, fell to pieces. (You can see a facsimile edition of *The Van Diemen's Land Edition of the Pickwick Papers* in the Tasmaniana Library.)

Perhaps, even if he was on a morally sticky wicket, Mr Dowling was operating on very sound logic. After all, what were they going to do to him? Transport him?

Malcolm
Campbell
—racer

A quiet street in Launceston's
Riverside is not where you'd
expect to find one of the world's best
motorcycle racers; but that's where
Malcolm Campbell lives.

H e started his long career in 1972, riding a couple of converted road bikes in club races at Symmons Plains and
Baskerville, and was soon at the top of the heap in local
events. Occasional visits here by mainland riders then showed Mal that he
could go at least as fast as they could (often on inferior machinery), and he
began making forays to mainland events.

By 1980 he was regularly on the podium in major events—especially
production bike races, which were among the glamour events of the time.
The following year saw him win the first round of the 500cc Australian
Road Racing Championship on a Suzuki, only to break his leg badly at
Bathurst soon after on a production Honda. After several months in hospital, he finished second in the Castrol six-hour production bike race and
won the New Zealand six-hour. It was during this period that he acquired
the reputation of being a demon qualifier. He also acquired the nickname

'Wally' (after a television chimpanzee), allegedly when team-mate Roger Heyes wrote 'Go bananas, Wally' on his speedometer to spur him on to greater efforts.

After a year in the doldrums with Suzuki in 1983, he accepted a Honda Australia contract, and won race after race, finally taking out the Swann Insurance Series on one of only three Honda RS 920Rs in the world.

In 1984 he managed to fall off a Grand Prix 500 Honda while doing a wheelstand on the lap of honour after winning a race in Malaysia ('I was stupid,' he says), and after several more crashes in the same year he rethought his whole approach to riding. He emerged from numerous hospital beds a more thoughtful and analytical racer. Where previously he might have 'ridden around' problems with the bike, now he was prepared to put in the time to get it set up properly.

It paid off in 1985, with an Australian Superbike Championship for Mal and Honda, and in the Swann Series, perhaps his most famous victory over Honda works rider Wayne Gardner in the wet at Oran Park. Gardner was on a full works 4-cylinder Honda, while Campbell was on a less powerful 3-cylinder model. After a poor start he hacked his way through the field until he caught Gardner, and the pair laid on a titanic race which Campbell won by about a wheel at the line. He won again at Surfers Paradise, setting the all-time lap record, and was noticed by Suzuki team manager Roberto Gallina, who earmarked him for a test session in Europe.

In 1986, after an Australian Grand Prix win at Bathurst and a further win in the Superbike International at Calder Park, his European test session happened. Gallina flew Campbell and wife Sue to Yugoslavia for tests on the new 4-cylinder 500 Grand Prix Suzuki. Campbell, however, knew that the bike was not competitive, and returned to Australia to sign with Team Honda Australia for a fifth season.

In 1987 he was the Australian Unlimited and Superbike champion, and had another international ride in the Le Mans 24-hour race, where he gave the revolutionary Honda NR750 oval-piston machine its world debut. (He also gave it its first race win, at Calder Park in the Swann series.)

The following year he astonished the Superbike World Championship regulars by placing his privately entered Honda on pole position (as fastest qualifier) for the Austrian round at Zeltweg and finishing fourth among the best superbike riders in the world. He also had his first Grand Prix ride, with the unconventional Elf-Honda at the French Grand Prix.

Back in the Southern Hemisphere, he again took the Australian Superbike championship and finished sixth in the prestigious Suzuka eight-hour race in Japan.

On a return visit to Europe for the Superbike round in Hungary in 1990, he yet again put his bike in pole position, this time finishing second outright. Amazingly, this was his last World Superbike ride.

He continued his winning ways through 1991 and 1992, eventually being inducted into Tasmania's Motor Sports Hall of Fame, and then took an 18-month layoff.

Those who thought Campbell had retired (he was now approaching 40) were in for a shock. On his return, he finished second in the six-round Malaysian Superbike Championship, and then dived into one of the sport's most competitive classes—600 Super Street. Although he didn't have the same heady levels of success as before, he was still highly competitive in a class full of people half his age and on bikes that were largely equal in performance. If you wanted to win, you still had to beat Mal Campbell. He would race for four more years, and had now been followed into the sport by his sons Scott and Kris.

Then in 1998 the sport that had given him so much, and to which he had given so much, took away his son Kris. He died in a crash at Symmons Plains during a riding clinic, and compared to this loss Malcolm felt that his own achievements over the previous 26 years added up to very little.

It's a view that any parent can understand; and yet Malcolm's career has been so admirable that it's hard to put it aside. It marks him as perhaps the best Australian rider not to get a full works ride on the world scene. What the records don't show is that he is, and always has been, the same person as when he started out—friendly, sportsmanlike, approachable and prepared to help others. When a job needed to be done, Malcolm was never afraid to pitch in and get his hands dirty. These are qualities that any good Australian parent would want to pass on to a son or daughter. That they are found in a person who has achieved so much makes them even more admirable.

In August 2000 Mal's contribution to Australian sport was recognised on a bigger stage when he was asked to carry the Olympic flame on part of its journey around Tasmania. While this may have been his slowest and shortest 'run', it's still unique recognition for a unique individual—and it's something of which he's justifiably proud.

Matthew Brady

The Old Woolpack Inn, at Breadalbane,
is a private house nowadays, but it has a
history that goes back a long way. It is almost
certainly the same building that was once
known as the Cocked Hat Inn; it was near
here, on Cocked Hat Hill, that Matthew Brady
the bushranger surrendered to John Batman,
saying that he didn't mind giving himself up
to a brave man and a gentleman, but he was
damned if he'd let the redcoats get him.

The visitor to Tasmania, hearing about Brady's Lake, Brady's Sugarloaf, Brady's Lookout (of which there are at least two), and the vessel *Matthew Brady*, would certainly expect the Brady in question to be an important person.

And important he certainly was. Probably alone among Tasmania's bushrangers, Matthew Brady acquired an almost Robin Hood-like status among the ordinary people of Tasmania in the early 1800s. Far from leaving a trail of death and despair behind him, Brady had the reputation of being unfailingly gentlemanly to his victims, especially the women, and stood out among his companions as a fair dealer (for a thief).

Brady arrived in Tasmania in 1820, sentenced to seven years penal servitude for forging a cheque to pay a debt. He started off doing 'easy time', but his attempts to escape landed him at Macquarie Harbour on the West Coast. This was the nastiest and remotest of Tasmania's penal settlements. It was here that he first emerged as a leader and that he met James McCabe. (Both were to have Derwent River ferries named after them in Robert Clifford's 'Bushranger' fleet, although McCabe deserved his immortality a lot less than Brady.)

In 1824 Brady, McCabe and five others escaped by commandeering a whaleboat, and over the next week sailed it around the south coast to the Derwent estuary—no easy voyage. Before they left, Brady had already taken command of the gang, preventing them mistreating the prison doctor.

Their efforts to survive on the run turned them into 'de facto' bushrangers. One of the first houses they robbed belonged to a Lieutenant Gunn of Old Beach. William Gunn was a giant of a man at nearly two metres tall, with a constitution to match, and he set out from that day to capture Brady and his gang.

The gang at first swelled in numbers, and then began to dwindle as its members were gradually caught and hanged, until the only ones left were Brady and McCabe. These two vanished briefly from view; they then returned on the scene and managed to keep the colony in a such a state of terror that in April 1825 Lieutenant-Governor Sir George Arthur offered a reward of '20 gallons of rum' (about 120 bottles!) for their capture. A week later Brady stuck a notice to the door of the Royal Oak Hotel at Crossmarch stating:

> It has caused Matthew Brady much concern that such a person known as Sir George Arthur is at large. Twenty Gallons of Rum will be given to any person that will deliver this person unto me. I also caution John Priest that I will hang him for his ill-treatment of Mrs Blackwell, at Newtown.

This was not Brady's only proclamation in this vein. He also made himself a lot of friends among the working class by threatening to hang anyone he caught mistreating servants. The gang now began to build up again, and went on a (fairly gentlemanly) rampage of robbery.

One of their associates at this time was Tom Kenton of Jericho, who joined them in their robberies but who was playing both sides. When he betrayed them, McCabe narrowly got away, and the police tied up Brady and left him with Kenton while they chased McCabe. Brady in turn escaped, sparing Kenton's life; but when he heard Kenton's version of the story, he was not impressed. He had not killed him for betrayal, but he swore to kill him for making himself appear heroic at Brady's expense.

McCabe only had a few months to live anyway; he was soon to be caught at Bothwell (through his own stupidity) and hanged.

The climax of Brady's career was a raid on the town of Sorell. First he and six companions stopped at Thornhill on Pittwater, where they robbed Mr Bethune and enjoyed a meal with him. They also accommodated Mr Bethune's brother Walter, who arrived for a visit the following day, and had another good feed. Then after dark they marched their captives through a storm to Sorell. They burst into the Sorell gaol and set the prisoners free, replacing them with the guards and their own captives. The gaol Governor, Laing, was wakened by the noise and called out Lieutenant Gunn (the leader of the troops in the gaol), who was staying in a house across the courtyard. Gunn rushed into action, and the bushrangers brought him down with a volley that smashed his right arm and hit him in the chest. (He survived, but lost his arm and was thereafter known as 'Wingy' Gunn. He also continued to hunt Matthew Brady.) Brady and his gang got away with several hours' start, by leaving a dummy 'guard' on duty to discourage anyone from following them.

In another of his bewilderingly fast trips up and down the island, Brady next came to notice in the Launceston area. Here he was keen to steal a ship, the *Glory*, to escape from Tasmania for good, but his gang did not have the stomach for it. He also declared his intention of taking a prisoner from the Launceston Gaol, but here he intended no kindness. He wanted to hang the prisoner Jeffries, the infamous cannibal and child-murderer who had been caught in the Cataract Gorge. Brady was to see more of him.

When he heard that Tom Kenton was working at the Cocked Hat Inn, he rode straight up to the door and demanded to see him. He confronted him with his lies (including two accusations of murder), and gave him five minutes to prepare for death. Kenton blustered that Brady wouldn't dare shoot him and tried to push his way out of the room. The witnesses believed that Brady would have let Kenton go if he had asked for mercy, but this was too much and he shot him in the head.

Two of the remaining faithful members of his gang were murdered by two other members swayed by the reward package (which at one time included £1500, a free pardon and a passage to England).

John Helder Wedge, one of his keenest pursuers, was disgusted by these murders, but continued to chase Brady, in company with another man called Sinclair and John Batman. Finally, unarmed and handicapped by an infected leg wound, Brady was captured by Batman on Cocked Hat Hill.

He now found himself in Launceston Gaol with the loathsome Jeffries, and was so revolted by him that he walked in chains to the ship for Hobart rather than ride in the cart with him.

There was a public outcry for mercy to be shown to Brady, but at his trial he pleaded guilty to each of the weird assortment of charges levelled at him (including one of which he was innocent) and was sentenced to death.

Brady and his surviving comrades were hanged in May 1826—again protesting, not at being hanged, but at having to share the scaffold with a wretch like Jeffries.

How to get there

The Old Woolpack Inn is on the left a few hundred metres from the airport roundabout at Breadalbane on the C402.

Until a few years ago the old gaol at Sorell was clearly visible from the main street, at the side of the Council Chambers. These chambers have now been extended; we have to trust to the farsightedness of the Sorell Council that the cells and doors of the old gaol have been stored away for later reconstruction...

Power
from the
people

Deep in the bush near Moorina, in
the State's northeast, is a power station that
predates every station operated by the Hydro.
Independently owned and operated, this
tiny station produces about 500–800 kilowatts
(enough to supply 200 houses), which it sells
to Aurora Energy, and which goes
into the State grid at Pioneer.

C ompared to the massive works at Poatina and the multiple huge penstocks plunging down the mountainside at other power stations, Moorina, with its single small pipeline, appears insignificant. Yet it has a significance, both historic and economic, that outweighs mere size.

The power station, which lives in a tin shed made from bush timber and corrugated iron, was built in 1908 by a mining company. The directors put their proposal to shareholders in 1906, reasoning that the booming mining industry could do with an electric power supply, but the shareholders rejected electricity in favour of their kerosene lamps and steam engines. When the directors put the same proposal the following year, the shareholders accepted it on the curious condition (given their previous reluctance) that it be finished before the next Annual General Meeting, in 1908.

And finished it was. Inside twelve months the Frome River was dammed, a water-race was constructed, a penstock falling 130 metres down the mountainside was built, and the station itself was finished. The generating equipment was fully installed and operating—no mean feat, since the three turbines and their alternators had to be shipped from Germany, landed at Boobyalla and carted by horses the remaining 50 kilometres to the Frome River. After the water had been used to generate power, it continued under pressure to Bradshaws Creek (now Pioneer) to work the alluvial tin mines.

Moorina Power Station has had its ups and downs since then. It's been struck by lightning, threatened by floods and bushfires and gone through a succession of owners and closure threats. (According to one of its present owners, the only reason it's still going is that they treat each day as if it will be their last.)

The most recent, and significant, ownership change came in 1988, when the station's then owners, Anglo-American Mining, decided to close it down and dismantle it. Its three long-term employees (who between them had operated the station for over 40 years) found themselves facing the dole and decided to 'buy themselves a job'. Tas King of Herrick, Mike Cook of Pioneer and Peter Dickson of Moorina invested their life savings in buying the station, and became its new owner/operators—now with an even keener interest in its long-term viability!

So far they've made it to the turn of the century, by working a punishing operation and maintenance schedule that keeps at least one of them on call 24 hours a day, 7 days a week—and they've now logged up over 70 years between them.

Thanks to their constant care, the machinery of the station is still doing just what it did nearly 100 years ago. How many modern machines, of any kind, will still be working at their present capacity in the year 2100?

How to get there

If you're coming from Scottsdale, turn left off the Tasman Highway (A3) at Moorina onto Frome Road. (It's a dirt road about 1 kilometre past the bridge over the Ringarooma River.) Stay on the Frome Road for about 2 kilometres until you reach a fork. Bear left, and about 1 kilometre further on, you'll come to some houses. The Moorina Power Station is down below the houses.

The Chinese in Tasmania

Today there are any number of well-known
and well-respected Chinese names in Tasmania,
especially in the business community. But at
the end of the 19th century, laws were passed
whose principal effect was to keep
them out of Tasmania.

T hese new immigration laws came about in 1887, at a
time when the Chinese were so numerous in the
northeast of the State that in areas like Branxholm
they outnumbered Europeans by 10:1! (Not that the numbers were ever
huge. Although they were the largest non-European ethnic community in
Tasmania in the 19th century, there were never more than 1500 of them.)

The main Chinese immigration was between 1875 and 1890. Some
arrived as 'mechanics' (a term which covered all manual workers, including carpenters), while others came as indentured servants. Some borrowed
from relatives to come, and paid the loans back from their wages. Many of
them came as an 'overflow' from the mainland gold rushes. Originally
brought in as cheap labour to work the alluvial tin fields of the northeast,
many soon branched out on their own and set themselves up as miners,
shopkeepers, market gardeners, cartage contractors and the like.

Tin represented a quarter of Tasmania's total exports in the 1880s. In the early days it was labour-intensive, and here the Chinese excelled. They were hard-working by nature and upbringing, and were prepared to do whatever it took to earn a living here. Many of them worked on the 'tribute' system—where the worker paid the owner of the mining lease a percentage for the right to use the lease—so the harder they worked, the better they did.

The Chinese also worked in the gold mines at Lefroy and Beaconsfield. Generally, wherever they worked they were well accepted, although there were isolated cases of harassment or confrontation between European and Chinese workers, generally based on the alleged willingness of the Chinese to work for a lower wage than the Europeans (although as they generally preferred to work on the tribute system, this may have been more of an excuse than a reason.)

The Chinese population began to decline from 1888 onwards, as a result of a recession in the price of tin coinciding with the new immigration laws of 1887.

By the time the alluvial tin was worked out (around 1897), operations became more machinery-dependent and capital-intensive, which meant that mines joined forces and grew ever larger. This also tended to squeeze out the Chinese, although some of them invested in mining ventures and others continued literally to scratch a living from the diggings.

In an industry where the same piece of land and the same pile of dirt might be gone over several times in search of 'paydirt', it is a high compliment to the Chinese that one retired miner pointed out: 'You couldn't prospect after them; they cleared every speck.' Conditions in China at the time were so awful that the migrants had every reason to work hard, either so that they could go home wealthy or so that they could stay here and set up new businesses. Many of them did become wealthy, and were key members of Launceston society at the turn of the 20th century. They were instrumental, among other things, in opening up the Cataract Gorge as a recreation centre.

Those who knew the Chinese on the mining leases were lavish in their praise of them, describing them as honest, industrious, innocent, peace-loving, community-minded and loyal to a fault. Well-known figures in the Chinese community in the late 18th and early 19th century included Maa Mon Chin, Billy Bow, Him Sheen, Ah Ling and Billy Ah Moy. Mrs Ah Moy was said to be the best-dressed woman in Tasmania.

Equally famous, but less illustrious, was Bo Wing, who used standover tactics and thieving in an attempt to set himself up as a kind of Chinese

'Godfather'. Naturally this made him unpopular, so it was no surprise that when he fell in a creek on the way home one night and lost his bag of belongings, it was discovered that 'somebody' had cut most of the way through the sapling bridge that had collapsed under him.

Bo Wing was an early recycler. He used to carry a stick with a pin in the end so that he could pick up cigarette butts, which he would later make into cigarettes for himself. He was also a very good billiard player and an excellent shot with a gun. His most notorious exploit came after his neighbour Roly Bonner accidentally burnt him out of his camp. Bonner felt that he should help him recoup his losses, so he wrote a petition in a notebook asking people to help Bo Wing financially, put some money in it himself and gave it to Bo Wing. This gentleman then set off with it to do the rounds of the mining camps and Launceston. (One account has him reaching Queenstown!) By the time his benefactors finally tired of him, he was alleged to have made £100—which would certainly have fitted his camp out in considerable style 100 years ago.

The Chinese brought much of their own culture with them, and loved to celebrate the Chinese New Year with fireworks and feasting—two activities that made them very popular with the European children (whom they loved anyway). The fireworks were paid for with a kind of gaming tax that they levied on gambling. A certain percentage of the turnover from games such as Fan Tan was always set aside; as they loved to gamble, the firework displays were spectacular. Another recreation, this one with a cultural significance, was roasting whole pigs in specially built 'pig ovens'. These were to be found not only around Chinese camps, but also in cemeteries, as they had a ceremonial role in Chinese funerals.

They enjoyed alcohol too—gin and schnapps being favoured tipples, while opium was the recreational drug of the time among the Chinese. According to one who was born in Weldborough in 1897, about 80% of them smoked opium.

Their religion came with them too. There were specially built Joss Houses at Weldborough, Branxholm and Garibaldi—the entire contents of the Weldborough Joss House, the largest of them all, were donated to the Queen Victoria Museum and Art Gallery in Launceston by the Chinese community in 1934. (It is still used as a place of worship.) This museum now has the finest collection of Chinese ceremonial artefacts in Australia. (The word 'Joss' simply means 'God'. It is derived from the Pidgin 'Deos', which in turn is from 'Deus', the Latin for 'God'.)

Little is left now of the Chinese camps in the northeast, but if you know where to look you can still find traces of habitation. A proper study was carried out by Helen Vivian in 1985 after some of the sites were ravaged by fossickers using bulldozers! She has now identified many of the sites with grid references, and her book shows exactly what is visible and what its significance is.

In the Moorina cemetery, for example, there is a grave with Chinese characters engraved on it, as well as a memorial to the Chinese dead; this memorial includes an oven for preparing food and burning papers—these being part of the Confucian tradition of honouring the dead. This little cemetery is worth visiting because of its delightfully peaceful site, on a grassy slope overlooking rolling farmland and forests. There are a number of Chinese graves, too, in the Gladstone cemetery, each distinguished by the memorial stone being at the foot of the grave.

In Fingal, the house of Jimmy Ah Foo, a successful market gardener and herbalist, is still standing, still occupied and still in good condition. Jimmy Ah Foo lived there until 1925, and it is now the best example in the State of a Chinese residence.

A curious footnote to Ms Vivian's research is that when she interviewed people who had lived among the Chinese early in the 20th century, two of them identified movie star Merle Oberon as having been born at Weldborough—both of them describing her as 'Lottie Chintock's daughter'! This is in contrast to the commonly held view that her birth in Tasmania was a publicity department invention to cover up illegitimate Eurasian ancestry.

Ship or shearing shed?

It might be supposed that in the early 1900s, mining in Tasmania would have been a pick-and-shovel affair; but in fact it was, for a time, quite mechanised. The problem with all mining, however, is that rarity usually equals value.

S o the amount of material recovered is often tiny compared to the amount that must be shifted to get it out. One attempt at a solution to this problem in the mineral-rich northeast of Tasmania was the tin dredge.

A tin dredge was something that looked like a monstrous cross between a shearing shed and a ship. That it floated, and that its boss was called 'Captain', was about all it had in common with a ship, although officially, that's what dredges were.

The dredge worked on the principle that tin was carried and deposited in rivers, so that was where it would be found. First, a dam was built; then the dredge was built to float on the dam. Some of these were truly monstrous machines—a typical one floated on two pontoons each as big as a Sydney–Hobart Yacht Race line honours winner, with a large tin shed housing the machinery on top. It pulled itself across the dam on cables, scouring away the bottom with a system of gradually lowering buckets. A dredge could, in theory at least, shift many thousands of cubic metres in a week in its (fantastically noisy) search for tin. It also brought up gold, silver, other metals and precious and semi-precious stones—when it was working properly. (An indication of the rarity of gold is that in 1907, when some 4000 tonnes of tin were found in Tasmania, the figure for gold was about 2 tonnes.)

Unfortunately the character of Tasmania's rivers and the way the tin was deposited made the dredges unprofitable. When a dredge hit a submerged log (of which Tasmania has more than enough), it would tip up and lose the tin it had already dredged up; and when it found isolated pockets of tin they were often in the form of 'pot-holes' that did not lend themselves to dredging. This resulted in vast amounts of unprofitable material having to be removed to get at them.

Nonetheless, the dredges survived and even enjoyed a revival after World War II, perhaps because the war had forced tin prices up and made them economical again. They ceased operations for good in the early 1970s.

A pontoon from one of these monsters can be seen beside the Ringarooma River, near a bridge about halfway between Pioneer and Gladstone. The Gladstone service station/store has a small picture gallery of dredges on its walls, and they can direct you to the derelict one. There is also an almost intact one at Doone Lagoon, apparently.

How to get there

To get to the Pioneer/Gladstone area, turn off the Tasman Highway (A3) roughly half-way between Derby and Weldborough, and take the B82 for Herrick and Pioneer. This is the Gladstone Road. On the way it's worth stopping at South Mount Cameron to check out the Blue Lakes. These lakes, which are only 50 metres from the road, were formed by mining kaolin (for whitening paper) and have a remarkable blue colour. They were the highlight of the day for our two boys when we visited them!

The Mysterious East

Eddystone
Point

Lighthouses the world over evoke in
people a variety of feelings—to the sailor
they symbolise safety, organisation, and help;
to the lay person they conjure up loneliness;
to the lighthouse keepers themselves they
call up memories of family life in often-
difficult circumstances; and to all of us
they symbolise strength and reliability in
the face of ferocious weather.

P laced where it is on the globe, Tasmania has more need of lighthouses than many other places, and it has 15 of them dotted around its rocky coast. Any of these are worth a visit, if you can reach them, to admire the workmanship with which they are put together, the enterprise it took to put them there, and the enormous seas with which they are often surrounded.

The lighthouse at Eddystone Point (named after the famous English headland of the same name) is a typical example. You get to it from the Scottsdale direction by turning off the Tasman Highway towards Herrick, Pioneer and Gladstone. At Gladstone you take the C843 (a good dirt road) for Anson's Bay, and just before you reach it go left on the C846 for Eddystone Point. This drive in itself is something of an education. Until you leave the bitumen you've often been driving through hills, bush and rainforest on twisty roads. Suddenly the land is flat and clear, and the road is relatively straight. There are big farms on either side, but they're completely unlike the rolling greenery around Scottsdale. And the soil is sandy, so sandy in fact, that a principal hazard on the old track used to be its disappearance under the drifting sand.

You can see the lighthouse from some distance off—it's as tall as a multi-storey building and visible from 27 kilometres out to sea—and you can hardly fail to be impressed. As you get closer, the scale of the place becomes even more impressive. The lighthouse stands at the end of a little line of houses, occupied according to the hierarchy of lighthouse keepers, and it dominates the whole coastline. Built in unpainted pink granite, with elegantly curved walls that are at least half a metre thick, it draws the visitor up to it like a magnet. When you go up the beautiful little stone steps to the door, you'll find that unfortunately it's locked; and these days the lighthouse is unmanned, so its secrets remain inside. But the coastline and the area around, the Mount William National Park, deserve a look.

Close to the lighthouse, for example, you'll find a little grave dated 1898. It's for Walter McFarlane Kirkwood, the infant son of a keeper. (Those were hazardous days, especially for people in isolated places. A later keeper was to lose both his sons to accidents.) A handwritten diary exists from 1898–1899, and it makes frequent reference to a keeper and 'the boys' going out after kangaroos and sometimes coming back with twenty-odd in a day. This is significant, since eight years later the entire staff was to be transferred elsewhere under a cloud that resulted largely from 'illegal possession of kangaroo skins'!

They don't seem to have made too much of a hole in the local population. If you check the sandy soil for footprints you'll find some that look as if they were made by a T-Rex; so the big forester kangaroos at any rate are still about.

Along the rocks by the sea you'll see where the granite for the lighthouse was taken from—you can tell by all the broken rocks with half-channels in them where the blasting charges went.

The Eddystone Light is there, on the easternmost point of Tasmania, to warn seafarers of the dangerous Victoria Rocks, Georges Rocks and Black Reef offshore, and to indicate the southernmost end of Banks Strait. The waters here have marked the end of many a ship. (In 1920 one of these, the schooner *Amelia J*, not only disappeared, but was apparently followed to her unknown end by an aeroplane that set out to search for her.)

It's a paradox that today, when the loneliness and tedium of being a lighthouse keeper could be dramatically relieved by communications technology, the same technology has given us the capacity to leave all the Tasmanian lights unmanned. Maybe in the future we won't even need the lighthouses themselves—which would be a pity, somehow.

The storm of the centuries

In Tasmania we all know what heavy rain is like. When you get 25 millimetres of rain in a day, that's heavy. Get twice that and it's really heavy. So how about twenty times that in a day?

T hat's what happened during the night of 21–22 March 1974 on the East Coast of Tasmania near St Helens. It was impossible to tell exactly how much rain there was, because in the places where it was heaviest the rain gauges overflowed; but the Weather Bureau's best estimate is at least 500 millimetres (or half a metre) in that single 24-hour period.

How did it happen? It was the same type of rain that accompanies thunderstorms, but it differed in one important respect. Unlike a thunderstorm, which drops a large amount of water and noise for a fairly short time and then moves on, these storms did not move.

The weather forecast didn't sound too threatening. It didn't even seem to mean much to the lay person—there was 'a strong low-level flow of moist air from the Tasman Sea, with light winds aloft ahead of a slow moving upper trough.' The origins of the moist air might have sounded a bit more sinister. There was a deepening depression off the coast of Queensland (which was to become Tropical Cyclone Alice), while in the Tasman Sea there was an anticyclone. Between them, these two produced the northeast flow of low-level moist air onto Tasmania.

The moist air was moving quite quickly over the relatively smooth sea until it reached the Tasmanian coastline. Here the lower layer was slowed down by the roughness of the terrain, and the air behind continued trying to push in, with the result that lots of moist air was pushed straight upwards in a forced convection current. When moist air rises its temperature falls and it typically becomes rain; as indeed it did in this case. Had there been higher winds up above, had air movements in general been different over the State, the storm would have kept moving; as it was, according to the Weather Bureau:

> '[the storms] appear to have remained almost stationary for many hours, the resulting rainfall producing severe local flooding and considerable flood damage.'

Naturally the rivers did not cope too well with having an additional half-metre of water dumped into them overnight. Both the Golden Fleece rivulet and Fern Tree Creeks washed away bridges, while two more bridges were lost near Scamander. Half a metre of water, incidentally, means an amount of water that would cover not just the river, but all the surrounding land, to the depth of half a metre!

Germantown and Cornwall had the worst of it, but as these were the places where the rain gauges overflowed, the highest officially recorded figure was the 377 millimetres at Cullentown.

To put this rainfall in perspective, there is a 'freak' rainfall figure for most States that they can expect to see about once every 50 years. The rainfall of March 1974 was two and half times as heavy as this 'once every 50 years' figure for Tasmania—and it occurred 45 years after the previous record rainfalls of 1929.

The Weather Bureau has estimated that the frequency of rains like these is in the hundreds of years—so it could be something like 500 years before we see their like again.

'This is a job an idiot could do... and you look like a natural for it!'

Mount Elephant, between Bicheno
and St Marys, on the East Coast of Tasmania,
is allegedly named for its resemblance to
an elephant. And there is one place, approaching
from the north, where the resemblance
is visible. The elephant in question looks
a little limp—more like a 'jellifant'.

Lew Bretz, proprietor of the Mount Elephant Pancake Barn at the top of Elephant Pass, is frequently asked how the mountain got its name (presumably by others who can't see the similarity), and delights in telling huge lies in his Louisiana drawl: 'Well, this is where the Tasmanian

Aboriginal hunters used to drive herds of elephants over the edge to kill them' is one. Another is the story about the circus in the 19th century that got its carts stuck on the track up the mountain and used its elephant to pull them, whereupon the elephant died of heat exhaustion, causing the locals to say: 'This is the place where the elephant passed [away].' Lew finds his customers endlessly gullible, especially when he introduces them to Pauline the gorilla. But that's another story.

It's an elderly real estate cliché that the three most important words in property are 'location, location, location'. Whoever wrote them should visit the Pancake Barn. Its location would be more appropriate for a fort than for commercial premises.

Approached from either side by the switchback Elephant Pass (which itself isn't the main road to anywhere), it has nothing to offer but itself. No souvenir shops, no craft stalls, and a line in car park signage that makes some people turn around and drive straight out again. When you exit the twisty road into the car park, and look around for a spot, this is what you're faced with (in three or four languages) if you attempt to park across one of the gates into the property:

> Don't even THINK about blocking these gates!
> Our elephants will stomp your wretched hire car down to the hubcaps. Thanks for cooperating.

This is repeated in German and French—the French adding an additional flourish about the car being 'as flat as one of our crêpes'—and in a fourth mystery tongue:

> No pa king U hi ka. Tenksa lot.

'I don't mind if they drive out again', says Lew. 'It weeds out the ones with no sense of humour and then we don't have to deal with them.' And 'deal with them' he does. If you've ever had a meal spoiled by uncontrolled kids, you'll be reassured by the note on the menu:

> ...the surcharge on rowdy children is charged against their parents, but at their option the child may instead be fed to the elephants. This saves you money and may be a popular choice with other diners, depending on the child. Our back yard is a good place for kids who need to be active, tinker with breakables or be noisily unhappy while not eating.

Quirkiness seems to be a requirement for ownership of the Barn, and Lew is no exception. The location was chosen by its original owner, the late, award-winning chef Joel Chartrain, who came here to escape from the rat-race and found that his European-style savoury and sweet crêpes made him a minor celebrity. The unusual architecture is due to a mixture of European heritage and lack of money. The great view, for example, is broken up by small windows because this was the only size of glass he could afford! M. Chartrain's recipes are still in use after two further owners, one of them a motorcycle-loving Dutchman who put up a sign on the Elephant Pass saying that Ducati owners were particularly welcome. This same man, Andreas Wyminga, allegedly told Lew 'This is a job an idiot could do...and you look like a natural for it.'

There are elephants everywhere too—on the logo, on the walls, on the shelves, and even on the restaurant floor in the form of two huge carved armchairs. Lew discourages children from fiddling with their tusks by assuring them gravely that the elephants will sneeze on them and cover them from head to foot with elephantine quantities of yecch. If they persist in being difficult he introduces them to Pauline, a small black gorilla toy who, he assures them, will follow them around and take a bite from their bum. (He also asks them not to let Pauline know that she bears no resemblance to him: 'She doesn't know she's adopted!')

The pancakes are excellent, and Lew and his family are far from being ogres. So far, in fact, that no-one here accepts tips. Instead they donate them to the Fred Hollows Foundation to save the sight of people in poor countries. The Pancake Barn has already donated $25,000 raised in this way, and has saved the sight of over 500 people who would otherwise be without it today. So when Lew pulls the wool over your kids' eyes, remember that he should be allowed a bit of latitude where eyes are concerned.

How to get there

The Pancake Barn is 8 kilometres south of St Marys, or 8 kilometres from the Tasman Highway, on the A4.

One of the world's top **beaches**
...and a spare

A beach that has been selected as one
(the only Australian one) of the world's top
ten is hardly a secret, you might think—
but one of the criteria by which *Outside*
magazine judged its top ten was privacy.

And Wineglass Bay is certainly private. It gets its name from its exquisitely curved shape, which the beach partly follows. What makes it special and secret, apart from its shape, its dazzling colour, the views it commands and the clear blue sea, is that you can't drive to it. If you want to see Wineglass Bay, you have to either reach it by sea, or walk.

It can take an hour or so to walk to the beach over the saddle between Mount Mayson and Mount Amos. You can take a leisurely walk up to the lookout at the saddle and see the beach from above, the classic view, or you can climb Mount Amos and get the 'adventurer's view' from up there. In any case, it's worth taking the little extra time and trouble to get to the beach itself and get your toes in the sand. As the judge from *Outside* said when he gave it top marks for privacy, 'The morning I spent there I was the only human in sight.'

He obviously wasn't there on the day when the Royal Yacht *Britannia* moored in the bay and the royal passengers came ashore for a silver service picnic on the beach (and then had to send a boat back for a silver cutlery canteen that had been left behind). Nor was he there on the day when it became a billionaires' playground. One fine day in 1999 a number of large and immensely expensive motor yachts arrived for a beach party of their own, and their billionaire owners went for an expensive paddle. It's a pleasant irony that some of these people spent fortunes and sailed halfway around the world to get a fleeting glimpse of something that we can enjoy at any time, that's been there since prehistory and that will still be there after we're all gone.

The view from the beach at Wineglass Bay is stunning too—a vista of granite coastline that includes the peaks of the Hazards and the Cape Tourville lighthouse. But there is at least one Tasmanian beach with a better view—Crescent Beach, on the Tasman Peninsula. This is another delightful spot, enclosed by a rocky bay and backed by enormous sand dunes, but the view out to sea, of Tasman Island and the huge seas of the Southern Ocean, is something else. Sliding down the sand dunes on boards is a popular pastime here, but beware—skulls have been cracked.

How to get there

Wineglass Bay is in the Freycinet National Park.
Turn off the A3 for Coles Bay and drive to the end of
the road (the C302). It's about 27 kilometres.

You have to walk to Crescent Beach, too. Follow the C347
south from Port Arthur and take the last road on the left before the
Remarkable Cave. It's called Dog Bark Road! It only takes 15 or
20 minutes to walk from the end of the road to the beach, which
unfortunately means it's not so private. You could see as many
as half a dozen other people on the beach...

A piece of Greece

Where would you expect to find a Greek
amphitheatre? In Greece, right? Wrong.
Just a few kilometres south of Swansea on the
Tasman Highway, on a property called 'Piermont,'
you'll find an amphitheatre that is no
less genuine-looking for having been
built well within living memory.

An amphitheatre, incidentally, is defined as a level semi-circular performing area surrounded by rising ground—with or without seats. 'Piermont', the house built by Robert Webber from local stone and Oyster Bay pine in 1827, has been known to seamen for years as an East Coast landmark. Today the property belongs to Dr Ruprecht Von Haniel Niethammer, a forester who spends most of his time in Patagonia and describes himself as an 'ecological refugee'. He coined this description after selling up his family estates in Bavaria to escape from the acid rain that was threatening his tree plantations. Searching the world for the perfect place to build a small resort, he found 'Piermont'. It now boasts several small but luxurious cottages (built, of course, from local stone and timber), an Argentinian barbecue and, of course, the amphitheatre.

The 50-metre amphitheatre, with seating of local stone, is set into the hillside looking out over Oyster Bay towards the Hazards, and has already hosted a large number of events. Orchestral performances, acrobatic troupes, weddings, the East Coast Festival—all these have been here, and taken advantage of its amazing location and its seating for hundreds of patrons.

When you sit on one of the stone rows of seats (or, if you're an extrovert, stand on the performing area), it's easy to feel yourself transported back several thousand years. The construction of the amphitheatre has blended so naturally into the ground that it looks like it's always been there.

If you'd like to see the amphitheatre, call at the Piermont house and ask the hosts, Peter and Heather Boulot, for permission.

How to get there

The turnoff to Piermont is on the seaward side
of the Tasman Highway a few kilometres south of
Swansea, and is well marked.

The coroner
who came to a sticky end

The discovery of a bag of beheaded
and mutilated human remains in a London
street in the mid-1850s is literally a world away
from the peace and quiet of Tasmania's East
Coast; but it is almost certain that the creator
of the Lisdillon salt works ended
up in just this way.

J ames Radcliff, a native of Northern Ireland, took up about 1000 hectares of land at Little Swanport in 1830, and called it Lisdillon (after a small town in County Westmeath.) Inside the next eight years, he built himself a stone farmhouse and a number of outbuildings and, a couple of kilometres south, the salt works itself. This included a boiling house, a windmill, another house, a store, a blacksmith's shop and various other buildings.

The salt water was pumped by windmill from the sea to the salt works proper. This was composed of two buildings, the lower of which was occupied by a wood-fired boiler for reducing the brine to salt, while the upper one was used for final drying and packaging. The boiler even provided under-floor heating for the drying room. While it was an efficient and well-designed salt works, it was not an especially profitable one—perhaps because the water close to the mouth of the Little Swanport River was not especially salty! The works closed down after three years.

Radcliff was aware that the salt works was unlikely to be a commercial success, and put it up for lease before returning to Ireland in 1838. When he came back in 1844 with his new wife, he put the whole Lisdillon property (by then about 3000 hectares) up for lease and they lived at Rheban, near Orford. The property was bought 10 years later by John Mitchell (no relation to the Irish rebel).

Radcliff's last visit to the British Isles, in 1856, was supposed to be a short one; but he never returned. Although the remains found near Waterloo Bridge were assumed to be his, they were never formally identified. In fact, his wife Anna did not accept the fact of his death for years afterward, and continued to meet every ship arriving from London in case he was on it. Curiously, one of the posts Radcliff held in the Little Swanport district was that of a coroner!

How to get there

The old salt works still exist as ruins and are worth
a visit because they're in a picturesque spot. You can find
them if you turn off the Tasman Highway 24 kilometres
south of Swansea onto Saltworks Road.

'There's no such thing as free water...'

Anyone who was living in Tasmania in the 1970s and 1980s probably believes that they witnessed the first major dispute over dams between the people and the government. And if you ever feel that government service is deteriorating because of newfangled ideas like 'user-pays', you're not the first.

But you're not right either. There was a dispute over both dams and the 'user-pays' principle as long ago as 1844—predating the Gordon-below-Franklin dam confrontation by 140 years. In the 1844 case no-one objected to the building of the dam itself. In fact, it did get partly built, and plans are afoot even now to finish it or build a new dam at the same site.

In 1840 the British Government approved the building, with convict labour, of a dam at Long Marsh on a northern branch of the Macquarie River (between Lake Leake and Tooms Lake), to irrigate the farming properties in the area. Some 250 convicts started work, and after building accommodation for themselves they started on the dam itself. After four years of hard labour at the quarry face and on the ground they succeeded in building two dam walls, each 18–20 metres high, which are still there today to the east and west of the Macquarie River. One man, Thomas Collins, was killed by a falling stone, and his grave can still be seen.

As the local landowners looked forward to the millions of litres of water they would shortly have, they had no idea that the good times of free convict labour were drawing to an end. In 1844 the Colonial Secretary decreed that from then on, convicts would have to be paid for their work. The farmers had no intention of paying for something that until now they had enjoyed for nothing, and work on the dam ceased abruptly. That's why there is a gap in the Long Marsh Dam, and that is why a good dam site has lain idle for 160 years.

There is every sign, however, that it will not lie idle forever. Due to the efforts of Northern Midlands Councillor David Downie (a farmer himself), new interest has been shown in the potential of the site. The original dam walls are not appropriate, so a new dam would have to be built about 200 metres downstream of the original site. This impoundment would hold 15 000 megalitres—about half the total annual rainfall for the catchment. The Hydro-Electric Commission quoted the cost at $4.5 million, but private quotes suggest much lower figures—closer to $1 million.

Councillor Downie's original plan was to raise the money for the building of a new dam by subscription from interested farmers. At the time of writing, a government grant of some $140 000 had been made for the first of the three stages of the dam's construction.

How to get there

You'd have to be keen to go looking for it, but if you insist, here's how. Get a copy of the 1:100 000 Land Tenure map of the area (Little Swanport). The dam is marked, and so are numerous roads. A word of warning—it's very easy to get 'bushed' in this type of country, so tell someone where you've gone, take a compass and be careful. (We couldn't find it at all, due to going there without a map, and with a set of directions that were more imaginative than informative!)

The question is...
Why?

If you had been in Midway Point on
28 April 1996, you might have seen a yellow
Volvo with a surfboard on top pull up, and a tall
young man with long blond hair go into the
newsagents' shop to buy a lighter.

I f you had been in Sorell the same day, you might have seen him drive down the street and turn right at the traffic lights, or you might have seen him when he stopped again to buy a bottle of sauce. If you had been at the Port Arthur Historic Site at lunchtime, you might have dropped into the Broad Arrow Cafe for a bite to eat—and you'd have seen him doing the same, quickly eating a large meal on the verandah.

And if you weren't at the Broad Arrow Cafe on that day, be thankful. Because when he finished his meal, the young man went inside, took an Armalite rifle from a sports bag and killed 12 people in 17 seconds. Even more bizarre was that shortly before eating his meal he had apparently already murdered two people whom he knew well.

His name was Martin Bryant, and for reasons that have still never been made clear, he set out on 28 April to carry out a series of acts that would make him the most hated person in Tasmania.

Martin Bryant was certainly an odd person, with an odd history—a misfit at school, at 29 years of age he had the intelligence of a child. He had been left a large house and a fortune by an eccentric heiress who died in a car crash, and had inherited a further quarter of a million dollars from the suicide of his father.

He liked to talk to people, but they didn't like talking to him because he had very little idea of what was appropriate conversation or behaviour. His solution to this problem was to take long plane journeys all over the world so that he could sit next to people who could not get away from him.

He also liked guns. In the boot of his car was an FN .308 self-loading rifle, a semi-automatic Daewoo shotgun and a very large supply of ammunition.

Bryant's family had had a shack on the Tasman Peninsula, and he had also spent considerable time at Copping with his benefactor, the Tattersall's heiress Helen Harvey. Bryant knew the area well, and he knew the Port Arthur Historic Site very well. But Martin didn't like Port Arthur. In fact, as he entered the site on 28 April this young millionaire complained about the price of admission. And he didn't like tourists—particularly, for some reason, Asian tourists.

But none of this does anything to explain his actions. The first person he shot was an Asian tourist. But thereafter he appeared to be completely indiscriminate—Caucasian, Asian, male, female, old, young, visitor, worker—all of these are represented in the sorry tally of his victims.

When he left the café, two minutes after he started shooting, there were 20 dead inside and 12 wounded. He then went out into the car park and murdered four more people in and around the buses.

The site was by now in a state of confusion. At one stage people were trying to get into the Broad Arrow Cafe to see what was happening (the common view being that it was a re-enactment of some kind). Elsewhere, visitors were being kept indoors by staff who had realised the extraordinary and incredible fact that a gunman was on the loose. The group of 70 or 80 people who had seen what was happening at the Broad Arrow set off up the road, running for cover and safety, as Bryant replaced the Armalite with the FN and set off up the road in his Volvo.

It was on the way up this road that he was to commit what was probably the worst of all his crimes. Nanette Mikac was running up the road for safety with her two small children Alannah, six, and Madeline, three. Bryant stopped his car, told Nanette to kneel down and killed both her and baby Madeline. Then he chased Alannah, who had run off the road and hidden behind a tree. He fired three times, finally killing her, and went back to his car.

He then drove up the road to the Port Arthur toll booth, where he commandeered a BMW after killing all its occupants with his rifle, and took off in the direction of Hobart. Stopping again at the General Store, he took a hostage, forced him to get into the boot of the BMW and then killed the man's female companion as she sat in the front of their Toyota Corolla.

When he arrived back at the Seascape Guest House, he took his hostage inside, handcuffed him to a solid object and went outside to begin shooting at cars on the main road from Hobart to Port Arthur. After he had hit several cars, wounding their occupants, the road was deliberately blocked by one of them to keep others out of danger. At this time he also set fire to the BMW, and at some stage during that evening killed his hostage. The owners of the Seascape Guest House, whom he knew well, he had already murdered on the way to Port Arthur.

The initially chaotic situation at the historic site had been managed for the first couple of hours by ordinary people—including staff, local State Emergency Service volunteers, voluntary ambulance officers and off-duty doctors and nurses. It is a measure of their skills, commitment and courage that no-one under the care of a site worker was shot, and none of those who were wounded subsequently died of their wounds—some of which were dreadful.

When the ambulances and helicopters began ferrying the wounded to the Royal Hobart Hospital, it was to an environment that was absolutely prepared. The hospital had just finished a massive exercise in which it dealt with 'Code Brown', an imaginary disaster like a major tour bus crash. So ready was it, in fact, that staff were actually waiting for the first casualties to arrive.

Meanwhile, Bryant had been contained at Seascape, and was virtually surrounded by police, including the Special Operations Group. However, they could get no closer than a couple of hundred metres under cover, and given the amount of weaponry he had (and had found in the house) a frontal assault would have been a disaster. A negotiator talked to him, trying to find out whether the hostages were still alive, until the batteries of the cordless phone Bryant was using went flat.

Eventually the dilemma was solved early next morning when he set fire to the house and ran from it with his clothing on fire. Like his victims, he was taken to the Royal Hobart Hospital, where he was treated for serious burns to the back and buttocks.

When he was charged with 72 crimes, including 35 murders, Bryant upset the survivors further by pleading not guilty—and by the weird habit he had of always laughing at authority. When he later changed his plea to guilty, there was a wave of relief across the State and the country as survivors realised they would not have to relive 28 April in court.

To those who had been there, and survived, Public Prosecutor Damian Bugg pointed out, among other things, that there was no need to feel guilty about not having 'confronted' the gunman. People had confronted him, and in every case had immediately been murdered. The terrifying, mindless speed of his attack had in any case left no time to do anything, while the sheer volume of noise was enough to rob anyone of the ability to think clearly. Damian Bugg also praised everyone who had been there, including many of the dead, for their coolness under fire and their courage in trying to shield or help others.

Martin Bryant is now in Risdon Prison, serving 35 life sentences for murder and 21 years on each of the other charges. He will never be released.

No-one who had anything to do with Port Arthur on 28 April will ever be the same again. Problems of every kind have emerged for the survivors, the helpers, the volunteers, the police and emergency services, and the friends and families of the dead. For them and for the rest of us, the fact that the gun laws have been drastically changed is little consolation. The real question is not how he was able to do it, but why he wanted to do it. And to that there may be no answer. He may not know. Or if he does know, he may not have the mental ability to tell.

Today the shell of the Broad Arrow Cafe is part of a beautiful, peaceful garden—a memorial to the dead. Behind it is a pool, engraved with lines by local poet Margaret Scott:

> May we who come to this garden
> Cherish life for the sake of those who died
> Cherish compassion for the sake of those who gave aid
> Cherish peace for the sake of those in pain

Also engraved at the monument are the names of those who died. The list itself is even more affecting than the terrible number, since each is a life and a person.

How to get there

Port Arthur is on the Arthur Highway (A9), which goes south from Sorell. It is well signposted.

Three
naked
outlaws

The Tasman Peninsula's remoteness and
general inaccessibility made it an ideal place
for the 19th-century penal colony at Port Arthur.
That it was fortified in many places by cliffs,
covered in thick bush and surrounded by a cool
ocean that was home to the great white
shark may also have helped.

But it had another factor in its favour. At Eaglehawk Neck, the whole peninsula narrows down to an isthmus just metres wide; so any escaping convict travelling by land had to cross it, and (in theory at least) was easily caught. For this reason Eaglehawk Neck was known as 'the key to the Peninsula.' One of the more famous early escape attempts starred a former show performer named Billy Hunt, who disguised himself as a large kangaroo and set out to hop across the isthmus in full view of the guards. Unfortunately for him—soldiers' rations being what they were, and soldiers being what they are—one of them announced that he was about to take a pot-shot at 'that big boomer' and Billy was forced to come out of character and speak to him, 'Don't shoot; I'm only Billy Hunt.' He was lucky not to have been shot by accident; it's not a good idea to shock someone with a gun.

The chances of escape were later reduced by a line of dogs posted across the Neck at a narrow point. Each dog had its own light, and the area in front of their barrel kennels was paved with crushed cockleshells to catch the light. Estimates of the numbers of these dogs vary from nine to 14. Their breeds were various, but they were uniformly vicious and were cunningly tied up so that although they couldn't tear lumps out of each other, they could do it to people trying to get through the line. They had names like Ajax, Achilles, Ugly Mug, Tear'em…

One sergeant was brave and stupid enough to attempt to run through the line of dogs—possibly for a bet. Presumably he lost the bet. He certainly lost a piece of his flesh.

What this meant to an escaping convict was that the sea was the only way across Eaglehawk Neck. The waters were said to be infested with sharks. There were also dogs on 'stages' out in Pirates Bay.

So the scene, when the escapee Martin Cash looked down on it in 1842, was far from encouraging. Still, he had slipped through these defences once before (a feat which had raised his stock considerably with the inmates of Port Arthur). This time he had already made his plans with his fellow escapees, Jones and Kavanagh. They intended to wade through the shallows of Eaglehawk Bay, quite close to the Neck.

Taking all his clothes off and tying them in a bundle on his head, Cash set off, as quietly as he could manage, to swim to the other side. Unfortunately (a word which attended many escape attempts) the weather was rough and a breaking wave snatched his clothing away. After a brief struggle he found himself alone but naked on the other side. He assumed that his friends had been killed by sharks (which had, in fact, happened to others before) until he heard them whispering on the shore, discussing his own drowning. When he showed himself to them, he was amazed to find that they were also completely naked, and that their clothes had joined his own on the way out to sea. Laughing out loud at this stage could have given them all away, but they did it anyway.

They then had to make their way up a steep, rocky hillside, covered in thorn bushes. By the time they had climbed 300 metres up this hillside in the dark, their bodies and feet were in such a state that they decided to wait for daylight.

When dawn came they watched the constables searching for them on the other side, and then set off inland until they reached a convict roadmenders' hut. This they stormed and the occupant found himself face to face with three naked outlaws, one with an axe he had picked up on the way in. Although he thought he was done for, the escapees meant him no harm; they just tied him to the central post, and supplied themselves with food and clothing from the stores. The result was that they were once again (tightly) dressed as convicts—but at least they had new boots on their tattered feet.

They would remain free for several months, supporting themselves as bushrangers, but eventually they were recaptured. Jones was hanged, and Cash and Kavanagh were sentenced to death. Reprieved by Queen Victoria, Cash and Kavanagh were transported to Norfolk Island (where Kavanagh was later hanged for a murder during an escape attempt). After serving this sentence Cash returned to Tasmania, got married and later went to New Zealand, where he became a policeman and at the same time ran several brothels!

When he returned to Tasmania to retire, Martin Cash would become a (fairly) respectable orchardist, and would end his days quietly on his farm at Montrose—a far cry from evading capture, wading shark-infested waters and carrying out robberies, both clothed and nude! He is buried at Cornelian Bay.

The position of the dog-line at Eaglehawk Neck is marked today by a life-size bronze statue of a dog, complete with lantern and barrel, just above the road as you cross the Neck itself. (This dog doesn't have such an intimidating name—as the sculpture was the late Nick Tanner's idea, the locals have named the dog 'Nick' in his honour.)

Moments from the Midlands

Illawarra
Church
and
Churchyard

Christ Church at Illawarra, near
Longford, has a number of claims to its
small amount of fame. It deserves, in fact,
to be better known than it is.

Built from ironstone and bluestone in 1841 by Edward Dumaresq, it was originally a school as well as a chapel. It was not until over 40 years later that it acquired its chancel (the area around the altar) and was consecrated. This chancel was replaced by the present one in 1910. The famous Australian impressionist artist Tom Roberts is buried in its churchyard; and the work of another equally well-known artist, Arthur Boyd, decorates the altar.

The Mount Ireh property around the church was the scene in 1982 of the world ploughing championships. Then the plains rang to the sound of tractors driven by competitors from 19 countries, all straining to plough the perfect furrow and take home the trophies. The Cairn of Peace, with its horse-drawn plough, was left as a symbol of a peaceful sporting contest. Ironically, in the nearby cemetery, Tom Roberts shares his resting place with a young casualty of the Vietnam War—a contest that was neither peaceful nor sporting, but which has intruded even into this quietest of rural scenes. (This young man's grave is marked out with large stones and has a cross of stones laid across its middle.)

The Illawarra Church's most recent share of the limelight came early in 2000. It was due to be closed on 19 February as part of a diocesan rationalisation process that saw 23 churches close their doors. Its congregation of 20 were joined by dedicated church-saver The Reverend Calvin Viney in their fight to save it from closure and sale. So far they have been successful.

How to get there

Illawarra Church is on the eastern side of the Illawarra Road (B52) between the Bass Highway and Longford. You can see it on a small hill—a stone church with an imposing spire and a red roof. There are two driveways, but only one is used. The cemetery is nestled among the trees near the church.

Formula One on wooden bridges!

Looking at the Formula One
cars of today, and looking at the
narrow roads around Longford, you'd
be hard pressed to imagine the two
working together. But in the 1950s
and 1960s, they did.

During the Northern Hemisphere winter, the Formula One circus used to make its way Down Under for the Tasman Cup, a series held in Australia and New Zealand. The races were held at several Australian and New Zealand circuits, but Longford after its first couple of years was always scheduled as part of the series.

In the early days the sort of cars that raced at Longford were real club cars—hotted up Morris Minors, Hillmans, Austins, MGs, Fords, little Fiats and a variety of specials. These ranged from total 'bitsas' like the 'Purple

Petrol Eater' to tiny rear-engined things with large motorcycle engines. All they had in common was the intention (not always fulfilled) of going fast.

The year 1953 saw the very first race meeting on the 7.2-kilometre Longford circuit, and only a year later it seemed as if the circuit's history might be very short. Shipping difficulties prevented the meeting from being held. But in 1955 it was back with a bang—the first international meeting for motorcycles saw a motorcycle set an absolute speed record for the circuit that was not to be broken by anything on two wheels or four for another three years. World Champion Geoff Duke, on his 4-cylinder 500 Gilera, went around in 2 minutes 54 seconds, for an average speed of nearly 149 kilometres per hour. His top speed through the 'flying mile' was some 220 kilometres per hour.

The waterfront jinx struck again in 1956, but from that year on there was a meeting every year until 1968. Longford at that time was the fastest and, many thought, the best racetrack in Australia—the only true road-racing circuit in the country, and one of only a few in the world.

In the late 1950s the exotic cars began to arrive—the blood-red Ferrari and Maseratis, the dark green Jaguars and Aston Martins, the Coopers and BRMs, and always at their heels, the pack of local 'specials'.

The world's oldest Grand Prix, the Australian Grand Prix, first came to Longford in 1959, supported in the program by the Australian Motorcycle TT. Now too, the big names began to arrive. Jack Brabham's new lap record in 1960 (8 seconds faster than the previous one) made Longford the fastest circuit in the Southern Hemisphere.

The next few years saw a steady trickle of international stars on both cars and motorcycles—world champions like Tom Phillis (works Honda), who took 29 seconds off the 250 lap record! Then there was John Surtees (world champion on two wheels and four), Kel Carruthers (Honda) and Jim Redman (Honda).

In cars, there were Roy Salvadori, Bruce McLaren, Denny Hulme, Chris Amon, Jim Clark, Graham Hill, Phil Hill, Jackie Stewart, Richard Attwood, Ricardo Rodriguez and Piers Courage, as well as many Australians who gave them a run for their substantial money—Lex Davison, Kevin Bartlett, Frank Gardner, Frank Matich, Bob Jane, John Youl, Spencer Martin…

Motor racing is dangerous, however, and in 1964 and 1965 four people died in crashes at the Longford circuit—Tim Mayer, Rocky Tresise, Robin D'Abrera and Denis Wing. This did little to endear either the sport or the circuit to their detractors.

In 1965 the last-ever motorcycle race was held at the circuit—and fittingly it was the Australian Motorcycle Grand Prix.

The meeting kept going for another three years, and at its swan song in 1968 it was hard to believe there would never be another race here. Bruce McLaren's cars appeared for the first time in Longford, and the unluckiest man in motor racing, Chris Amon, took his fabulous works Ferrari 330P4 sports car around in a new absolute circuit record time of 2 minutes, 12.6 seconds, for an average speed of 195 kilometres per hour. On the flying mile his V12 engine shrieked up to 291 kilometres per hour. This lap record would now stand for all time (though, curiously, the flying mile speed would not).

The 1968 meeting was a strange mixture. The racing was superb, but the heavens opened and half-flooded the track. At the same time, the local arsonists set fire to the King's Bridge. The previous year, someone had burned down a barn with 13 000 bales of hay in it on the property of Ron McKinnon (President of the Longford Motor Racing Association). The trains, too, caused disruptions, as they had to cross the racetrack; and when they did, races had to be stopped and run in two legs.

The committee, or some of them, knew that this was their last meeting. It was impossible to sustain the expenses of running an international meeting, and it was very expensive to keep the circuit in the kind of repair that international motor racing now demanded—especially a circuit that contained not one, but two wooden bridges.

So what was it like to drive around the circuit? First, you have to find the start. As you approach from the small town of Perth, you pass the C531 on your right and you're on the start-finish straight. The highway now bears away to the right towards an 'accident black spot' intersection, while the racetrack used to plunge down to the left. Here's a lap of the 7.2-kilometre track as it used to be:

From the start you accelerate hard down the start-finish straight and through its two fast kinks towards the left-right 'ess' under the railway viaduct—this is a set of bends that would give a modern track designer nightmares, with solid brick walls on both sides of the track (which itself is only a few metres wide). From here, it's another flat-out blast down a tree-lined straight towards a wooden bridge over the South Esk River, and off towards the right-hand Longford Corner, by the Country Club Hotel. Tannery Straight rushes off over a level crossing and continues for over a kilometre towards the right-hand Tannery corner. This leads to a short straight, then the Long Bridge (back over the river) and the tricky right at Newry Corner that leads up onto the flying mile—1.7 kilometres of flat-out straight, ending in the very tight Mountford Corner (C531) that leads you back onto the start-finish straight.

Unfortunately you can no longer drive right around the track—if you attempt it you'll end up in the South Esk River (twice)—but parts of it still survive, and other bits can be found if you know where to look.

The flying mile was last used for competition quite recently, in the inaugural Targa Tasmania in 1992, when Chas Kelly of Devonport stoked his Ferrari F40 up to 302 kilometres per hour. This enormous speed, and his efforts to get the red projectile stopped at the end of the flying mile, may have contributed to the abandonment of the stage in subsequent years!

Perhaps the best way to get a sense of what the track was like during its Grand Prix days is to visit the Country Club Hotel, where the Grand Prix Bar is constructed from the timbers of the King's Bridge (which was just down the road) and the whole bar and lounge are given over to displays of Longford in its heyday.

The new roads that bypass Longford, the demolition of the bridges and the placing of a hydro-electric sub-station in the middle of the old road near Newry Corner suggest that governments are not as committed to motor racing as they used to be; they certainly have the effect of making sure that the circuit will never reopen.

It's sad to see something so important and historic broken up, almost vandalised, into so many little pieces. Perhaps it's better not to look for the bits, but to remember the glory days when the howl of grand prix engines dominated the March long weekend. These days, Targa Tasmania does its bit, running a special stage around the streets of Longford. It's not the same, but perhaps it is creating its own bit of history.

Planned
down
under

If you're driving down from the
Great Lake towards Longford, you'll
find yourself on the mountain hairpins
of the Poatina Hill. When you come to the
end of the hairpins, and the road starts to
straighten out, you will see on your right a
building (marked 'Poatina Power Station')
in an electrical transformer yard.

T his building houses the lift shaft that leads down to the actual Poatina Power Station. If you drive in off the road you'll also see a massive pipeline plunging down the mountain above you.

But you won't see the power station because it's under your feet—150 metres under the ground is a vast, cathedral-like cavern (that's what 'Poatina' means in the Tasmanian Aboriginal language) which is home to half a dozen 50-megawatt generators, capable of producing 12% of Tasmania's electricity. If you drive a kilometre down the hill you can turn off to the left and go another kilometre to a small park. Here you can see the entrance to the power station yawning in the hillside like the mouth of Hades, and around it a pleasant, manicured area with fountains, power station memorabilia and a very 'hydro-electric' looking barbecue, complete with two sinks.

The cavern was excavated and the power station was built between 1957 and 1964 by what was then known as the Hydro-Electric Commission. At a time when the Snowy Mountains Scheme in Victoria was grabbing headlines all over the world for engineering innovation and enormous capacity, this Tasmanian power station was hiding its light under several million tonnes of rock. However, it was a match for the Snowy Mountains Scheme in both ingenuity and capacity—and because of the quantity of water available, its output was twice as high.

The decision to build the Poatina Power Station was a bold one in many different ways. The water from the Great Lake had, until 1957, flowed south, to drive the Shannon and Waddamana power stations. With the 'Hydro's' ever-developing civil and electrical engineering skill at an all-time high, it was realised that the sensible direction for the water to flow was north, towards Launceston. If this were done, it would be possible to take advantage of a huge fall of water, straight down the face of the Great Western Tiers. The only obstacle was the Western Tiers themselves...

To deal with the problem of getting the water from the Great Lake to the new power station, Hydro engineers had to dig a tunnel 6 kilometres long from the Great Lake out to the edge of the Tiers. From here, the water would flow down a 3-metre diameter penstock (pipe) to a point directly above the station, and would then drop vertically for 150 metres to the waiting turbines. In fact, the technology to build this new pipeline had only recently become available at enormous expense; and it was to avoid having to build a further 3 kilometres of pipeline that the decision was made to put the power station so far underground! Another tunnel would take the water from the turbines a further 4.5 kilometres underground before emerging into a canal for its final trip to the Macquarie/South Esk river system.

The people who built these engineering wonders needed somewhere to live, so the Hydro did what it had always done in the past—built a village for them. Partly prefabricated, partly permanent, the Poatina village was to be home first to the 2500 construction workers and then to the permanent workforce of the power station. It eventually had its own shopping centre, church, school, cinema, swimming pool, cricket/football ground and golf course. Large parts of it have been rehabilitated, but the surviving part (you can turn off to it at the bottom of Poatina Hill) is still there, and now belongs to Fusion Australia, who use it as a retreat and convention centre. The visitor is greeted by 'G'DAY' written in bricks on the hillside. Another thing you may notice as you drive around the streets of Poatina, apart from the emus, is the staggering number of BMC/Leyland 'Minis' you'll see. The local garage proprietor is a mini enthusiast and runs 'Ryan's Minicar Rentals'. He has a dozen parked out the front at a time and there seem to be a few other mini freaks around the town—minis can be seen in the driveways and carports of several houses.

If you're visiting the area, have a look around for fossils. In 1989 David Castle, a Launceston student on a field trip, found a 2.5-centimetre fossil of a horseshoe crab in a cutting by the roadside on the Poatina Hill. He was then launched into palaeontological stardom when his superiors produced a paper for the Royal Society of Tasmania (a body, incidentally, which was another of the contributions of Lady Jane and Sir John Franklin to Tasmanian culture). The little crab was found in the Jackey Shale where it had been exposed by roadbuilding, and had lain there rather longer than the road—over 250 million years. It was the first time this genus had been found, not only in Tasmania but in the Southern Hemisphere. The discovery showed for the first time that the crab could be found in rocks deposited in a high-latitude, cold-weather environment.

How to get there

If you're coming from the direction of the Midland Highway you can see the pipeline on the mountainside long before you get there. You can approach the mountains by any of several routes (e.g. via Longford and Cressy, via Powranna, or via Campbell Town), but the road you eventually want, for Poatina and the power station, is the B51—the Poatina Highway. The power station is about 3 kilometres uphill from the village turnoff, and the transformer yard is a kilometre further up.

In the past you could do a tour of the power station, but the risk of accident and litigation has put paid to that. You can, however, have a picnic or barbecue at the tunnel entrance grounds, as long as you do it on a normal working day.

Ghoulies
and
ghosties
and long-leggity
beasties...
and bunyips

Tasmania being generally thought
of as the most water-rich state in Australia,
it would be surprising if we didn't have
a few monsters in the closet.

With a lake the size of the Great Lake, and another the depth of Lake St Clair, there is plenty of scope for the active imagination to draw up blueprints for submarine horrors lurking out there in the mists.

Loch Ness has a way of grabbing all the monster-related headlines, but if the Tasmanian Bunyip had had a better public relations officer in the middle of the 19th century, Nessie would not have had it all her own way.

What is curious about the sightings of the Tasmanian Bunyip is how similar they are to one another, and how reputable some of the witnesses are—just as we also see with the thylacine (Tasmanian tiger). One witness, for example, was Charles Gould, government geologist and son of the ornithologist John Gould. The animal seen in the water (mostly at Great Lake and Lake Tiberias, which are not exactly adjoining waterways) is often said to be about 1.5 metres long, or as big as a large dog, and to have a head like a dog. Tapering hindquarters are sometimes mentioned as well.

If the above sounds like a seal to you, you're not alone. It would have been something of a feat of navigation for a seal to get there, but it could have happened. And if a seal could get there, aren't there other mammals in the sea that might have done so as well, given that whales and seals have been seen at New Norfolk, and sharks at Cornelian Bay?

Other theories include the usual 'survivor from the dinosaur era', 'half-man, half-beast' and supernatural phenomena of one kind or another; although suggestions put forward by sceptics to explain the sightings usually invoke the name of the Cascade or Boags breweries.

Some of the more off-the-wall sightings included 'floating logs' that suddenly swam away, sea-serpents with multiple humps and even dry-land tracks of two-legged creatures that may or may not have been related to the alleged submariners described above.

The 1930s were a productive period for sightings, and the people who had them can now rest easier in their beds—in the 1980s the 50-year-old skeleton of a saltwater crocodile was found in the central highlands. It was 2 metres long, it had a head that might be construed as dog-like (if you associate with Irish Wolfhounds) and it had a long, tapering tail. How it got there is another matter, but it would certainly explain some of the sightings—especially the mysteriously mobile logs.

The multiple-humped creatures can apparently be explained fairly easily by studying the habits of the platypus, which sometimes swims in groups in line astern, thereby creating the impression of a single large animal.

Rather less easy to explain is the behemoth in the Great Lake that allegedly sank the boat of two fishermen. This thing had eyes like saucers, a jagged back (which ripped the bottom out of the boat) and a 2-metre mane. It was over 6 metres long, and could reach, while carrying a dinghy and two men on its back, the curiously exact speed of 17 knots. The truth of this story can perhaps be guessed at by the tellers' insistence on remaining anonymous!

Two other fishermen (both accountants—a profession not known for its imagination!) claimed to have seen an eel-like thing 20 metres long and a third of a metre thick at Lake King William. There has also been a recent sighting of something similar at Lake St Clair—and a collision with a boat.

During the 1980s, two tourists on the shores of Lake Dulverton, outside Oatlands (and just over the hill from Lake Tiberias), were astonished to see a two-legged beastie over 2 metres tall striding towards them out of the shallows of the Lake. They didn't hang around long enough to be told that the sight of water in the Lake was perhaps even more astonishing. (At the time of writing it has water again. Maybe the 'Strider of the Shallows' will return.)

An obvious explanation for some of the sightings, but one that no-one has yet offered, is that the Tasmanian tiger has taken to the water to escape extinction. It's a theory that awaits a later scholar.

The secret town of Bothwell

Bothwell is another of those places that isn't really 'on the way to' anywhere except the lakes, and yet it is 'somewhere' in its own right. The centre of a large farming community, it is a long-established town with a considerable history.

U ntil quite recently the eastern approach to the town was lined with 110 pine trees, to commemorate the men from the district who went to the Great War. These trees were removed when they were considered to be dangerous. However, a monument to the war dead remains as a unique bluestone/granite/bronze sundial in the park at the centre of town. Made by Gundersons of Brisbane in a style modelled on ancient Greek sundials, it bears on its sides the names of the war dead and the inscription:

Municipality of Bothwell
In glorious memory of those men of
the district who gave their lives in the
Great War 1914–1919

Apart from its fame as the home for several years of John Mitchel (see page 172), and for many years of Grote Reber (see page 170), Bothwell can also claim to be the home of the oldest golf course in the Southern Hemisphere. Golf was played on the Ratho property as early as 1839—and it is possible that the course at Ratho is even older than the Royal Calcutta Golf Course, currently the oldest (1826) outside the United Kingdom.

A round of golf at the Bothwell Golf Club is an interesting experience. Rather than the precision mowing of courses like Royal Hobart, local sheep do the job of keeping the grass down. They are kept off the greens by wire fences, and if you hit one of these fences you can have another shot without penalty. Unfortunately three of the original holes were lost to the construction of the new bridge into Bothwell, and players no longer have to run the narrow gauntlet of big trees on one side and sheep pens on the other when teeing off on the seventh hole. To slice here was disastrous, and possibly personally dangerous if the ball came back out of the trees. To hook was catastrophic, and could condemn the hooker to savage and laborious chipping to get out of the sheep pens. Nonetheless, it is a serious golf course, and hosts the Highland Championship for 120 contestants every year.

It is fitting that the home of the oldest course in the Southern Hemisphere should also house a golf museum. You'll find this in a charming stone building not far from the memorial sundial, on the Dennistoun Road. Here you'll see some really ancient clubs, 'featheries' (feather-filled golf balls) and decades of golfing memorabilia. When you emerge you'll be able to use words like 'Mashie Niblick', 'Putting Cleek' and 'Baffy' as if you know what they mean.

How to get there

···

Bothwell is 25 kilometres from Melton Mowbray on the A5.

(If you're interested in sundials, there is another one perched
half-way up the wall on the corner of 43 Brisbane Street, Launceston.
Ironically, given that it's on a Masonic Hall, it doesn't give the correct time.
This is because its latitude is set for Launceston in Cornwall!)

···

Steppes
and
stones

About 34 kilometres north of Bothwell
on the Lake Highway, and just before you
reach the Steppes State Reserve, you'll see
a sign that reads 'Steppes Sculptures 300m.'
If you turn off the road into the car
park, you'll see…not much.

But follow the winding track and you'll find yourself in
a circle of 12 standing stones, some as tall as you, and
each bearing a bronze relief sculpture of a Tasmanian
bush scene. The scenes include indigenous animals such as the platypus,
snake, echidna, possum, Tasmanian tiger, an Aboriginal scene, a stockman
with cattle and several different birds, including an eagle. The centrepiece
of this strange, Stonehenge-like circle is a large rock, like a table, with a
near life-size bronze wombat on it.

A plaque in the centre reads:

The Steppes Stones
Dedicated to those who share in the love and care
of the Highlands of Tasmania from the past to the future.
Concept and sculptures by Stephen Walker A.M.

As a gift to Tasmania from the sculptor and his family.
Inaugurated by Vincent Serventy A.M.
28 November 1992.

(It is unfortunate that for some people the community gift is not enough, and they demand an individual one for themselves. Several times the bronze wombat has been stolen from the centrepiece and has had to be replaced.)

Behind the stones, the track goes on into the bush, and leads via an easy and pleasant 10-minute walk to the Steppes Homestead—the former home of James Wilson and his family. There are a number of charming old buildings here, including a log cabin bakehouse, with a truly enormous oven and chimney, dating from the 19th century. Wilson named the area 'Steppes', not after the arctic area with which it has quite a lot in common, but after a small town in Scotland!

From 1863 James Wilson was the superintendent of the South Longford Police Division, and the Steppes Homestead was its headquarters. (He was the man who first stocked the Great Lake with brown trout, carrying the trout fry up there in billycans on horseback.)

In his days as a policeman he used to bring mail up from Hunterson for the highland folk. This tradition was carried on after his retirement from the police, when the Steppes Homestead became the Steppes Post Office, with his wife Jessie acting as postmistress for 30 years. Their daughter Madge, also a Steppes postmistress for 30 years, was a wonderful wood carver, whose work can be seen at St Michael and All Angels Church in Bothwell. Indeed, the homestead itself was used for interdenominational church services long before the churches in Bothwell were built.

It was Madge Wilson, a true nature enthusiast and pioneer conservationist, who donated the Steppes Homestead and lands to the National Parks and Wildlife Service. The 48-hectare area is now known as the Steppes State Reserve.

As you drive on up the road in the direction of the Great Lake, you may be struck by the width and quality of the road. This section, at least, has always been wide to accommodate the droving of the big mobs of sheep and cattle that are brought up to the highlands for summer pasture.

Our
pioneer
radio-
astronomer

When we accept and use information about
the solar system, the galaxy and the universe,
we do so in the same way that we accept other
information from outside our own experience—
we assume that it comes from a reliable
source, and we take it for granted.

T he source of much of that information is the radio
telescope. But who first thought of building a dish to
capture radio waves from the stars?

The man who built the world's first radio telescope now lives in
Bothwell, Tasmania. Grote Reber was a 21-year-old student living in
Wheaton, Illinois, when he read in 1932 that Karl Jansky had discovered
radio waves that came from the stars. (Jansky worked for Bell Telephone
Laboratories, and was looking for the source of some annoying static.)

Although this discovery made the front page of the *New York Times*,
Reber was the only person on earth who grasped its importance. He set

to work and by 1937 he had built a working radio telescope just over 9 metres in diameter in his own garden. By the following year he was receiving radio waves, and for several years he was the world's only radio-astronomer. He published his results during World War II. After the war and its enforced exploration of microwave technology for radar and the like, radio astronomy was ready to take off.

From the USA he moved first to Hawaii, and then to Australia to work with the CSIRO. His reason for moving to Tasmania was that he now had an interest in long-wave radiation, and Tasmania is one of the few places on earth where electromagnetic waves with a wavelength greater than 30 metres can get through the ionosphere (the outer regions of the Earth's atmosphere). He had been assured by other astronomers that research into these long waves would be a waste of time, but he ignored their assurances and got to work.

During his working life Dr Reber divided his time between Tasmania and the USA. Today he lives in retirement in perhaps the most unusual house in Bothwell—a solar-powered dwelling that he built himself, prefabricating it and bringing the components to the site in Michael Street. His house and substantial garages reflect his other interests—energy efficiency in both housing and vehicles.

From here he can see the huge sky of Bothwell, and look out towards 'Dennistoun', where in the 1960s he built another radio telescope—a 1 kilometre diameter, 192-dipole array (3 kilometres from the nearest power lines, to reduce interference). This was specifically designed to make observations on the 144-metre wavelength, and from these observations he was able to make a 'radio map' of the entire southern sky.

The
honourable
escapee

Three kilometres out of Bothwell on the
road towards Lake Sorell and Lake Crescent,
you will find Nant Lane on your left. If you
turn into Nant Lane and drive down it past the
sandstone Nant homestead on your left and
Nant Mill on your right, you will come
to a fork with a gate to the right.

T hrough this gate you can see the rear of a cottage that
looks out alone over the plains and valleys leading up
towards the Central Highlands. If you go 100 metres or
so up this road you can get a look at the front. Unfortunately, at the time
of writing, the cottage, which looks fine from a distance, is in a state of such
disrepair that the front wall seems likely to fall down quite soon.

This is Mitchel's Cottage (also called Nant Cottage, presumably for ease
of identification!), named after the 'Young Irelander' John Mitchel, who in
1848 was transported for 14 years (to an unspecified place, but in fact to
Van Diemen's Land) for 'Treason Felony'.

Until about three years before this date, Mitchel had been a solicitor in
Banbridge, Northern Ireland, and when he was in Newry on business he
would often meet his oldest and closest friend John Martin—with whom
he was later destined to live at Bothwell.

Charles Gavan Duffy (subsequently Premier of Victoria!) invited him to
Dublin to join the staff of *The Nation* as a journalist in 1845. In 1847, infu-
riated by the Potato Famine and impatient with Duffy's soft attitude (he

called him 'Give-in' Duffy), he resigned to set up his own paper, the *United Irishman*, which advocated violent resistance to British rule. (During the Famine, absentee English landlords grew rich on the boatloads of grain that left Ireland while its people starved on a diet of blighted potatoes.)

In 1848 a retroactive Act was passed in the English Parliament, which allowed Mitchel to be prosecuted and sentenced for his inflammatory writings. He took 14 months to arrive in Tasmania, travelling via a succession of ships and prisons in Bermuda, Pernambuco and Cape Town. By the time he arrived, half a dozen of his prominent associates in the Young Ireland movement were already here—William Smith O'Brien, Thomas Francis Meagher, Patrick O'Donoghue, Terence Bellew McManus, Kevin O'Doherty and John Martin. They had been asked for their parole (their word that they would not try to escape), and all but O'Brien had given it. The parolees could live free, but in separate districts 50 or 60 kilometres apart. This was no great hindrance:

> It seems the three rebels whose dungeon-districts all touch Lake Sorell are in the habit of meeting almost every week at those lakes, which is against the rule, to be sure, but authorities connive at it—thinking probably that no great or immediate harm can accrue to the British Empire thereby.

O'Brien was confined at first on Maria Island and later moved to Port Arthur, where his cottage still stands.

Mitchel was no doubt grateful that he was not required to live in 'that metropolis of murderers and university of burglary and all subter-human abomination, Hobart Town.' Instead he moved up to Bothwell and stayed in a house in the town with John Martin. When his wife Jenny and their children joined him a year later from Ireland, they moved into Nant Cottage.

The first escape took place in 1852, when Meagher withdrew his parole and made his way to America. Further escapes were foreshadowed when Pat 'Nicaragua' Smyth arrived in Tasmania in 1853 to rescue as many of the Young Irelanders as he could. Smith O'Brien, who had by now given his parole and was living at New Norfolk, said the only decent way to do it was to withdraw one's parole in the magistrate's office, provide an opportunity to be arrested and then leave. Smith O'Brien himself was urged to go, but said Mitchel would be more at home in America than he would.

Mitchel was very serious about matters of honour, and agreed with O'Brien about the right way to do things; but he saw nothing wrong with laying the groundwork in the form of plans and bribes, while still on parole.

To this end, he bought Donald, one of the best horses in the district—'a white horse, half Arab, full of game and endurance'. The amusing thing about Donald was that he bought him from the local Police Magistrate, Mr Davis. This was to cause Davis some embarrassment in the future.

The original plan was that Mitchel and Martin would escape together, with Nicaragua Smyth standing by with five men in case of trouble. They would then ride to Spring Bay (Orford) to board the *Waterlily*, whose captain had agreed to run down or sink the local police boat if necessary. However, they soon discovered that their plot was 'blown to the moon'. Extra constables had been placed on duty, and both the *Waterlily* and Mitchel were under surveillance.

Aborting the plan, Smyth went to Spring Bay to send the ship off, and was taken for Mitchel and arrested. This, and the guard placed on his house, greatly annoyed Mitchel, who considered it a slur on his character. As far as he was concerned, the British authorities still had his parole.

Two months later, when a Sydney-bound ship was in Hobart, they tried again. This time, after setting off from the cottage for Bothwell, they met Mitchel's son galloping back from Hobart to say that the ship had already sailed. However, they carried on. Asking a constable to hold their horses, they strode into the Magistrate's office (next to the Bothwell Post Office) and Mitchel surrendered his ticket of leave as Smyth toyed with the pistol in his belt. While Mr Davis dithered, they galloped off down the street—Mitchel on his own horse Fleur-de-Lis, and Smyth on Donald. Some distance from Bothwell they exchanged clothes and horses, and Smyth rode Mitchel's horse to Nant Cottage.

Mitchel had decided to head north, where there were more Irish, and he was guided this way over the following weeks by a number of brave men, among whom was the son of another magistrate!

Nicaragua Smyth, meanwhile, had left a false trail, leaving Mitchel's horse 'reeking of sweat' in the stable at Oatlands, asking loudly about hiring a horse to ride to Spring Bay, and then slipping quietly up to Launceston.

Mitchel, in hiding at Westbury, was entertained to hear that when Mr Davis dismissed the constable who had held the horses, the constable got drunk and asked the pub to cheer for Mitchel.

> It is not true that this poor fellow was bribed; but I wish he had been; for it is now clear he was open to a bribe, wanted a bribe, and deserved a bribe.

Through a mixture of floods, misunderstandings and plain bad luck,

Mitchel then contrived to miss not one, but three ships—the *Don Juan*, which was to meet him between West Head and Badger Head (just west of the mouth of the Tamar River); the *Wave*, which was to take him as a Mr Miller, and the steamer *Clarence*, which he was to board as a priest, Father McNamara (a particularly bold disguise as Mitchel was not a Catholic). This last attempt involved rowing from Launceston to Kelso and back again, to try to board the ship off George Town.

Having been on the run and in hiding for weeks, he now decided to take the coach to Hobart. This time he was the Reverend Mr Blake—an unusual cleric who carried a pistol in the pocket of his soutane. He knew it was a good disguise when his old friend Kevin O'Doherty got on the coach eight kilometres from Hobart and sat in the seat opposite without recognising him!

Even Nicaragua Smyth, now in Hobart, did not recognise him. Smyth was able to tell him that the Magistrate was still suffering after his escape: 'Many will continue to believe that I bought not the horse, but the owner', he reported gleefully.

Mitchel sailed on the *Emma* for Sydney on 19 July 1853 as Mr Wright. Mrs Mitchel and their children were on the same vessel, but Mitchel did not speak to her, as he 'had not been introduced.'

His departure coincided with the end of transportation, a subject which exercised his mind and showed up some of his more extreme views:

> …in a generation or two, then, the convict taint may be well-nigh worn out of the population; and those most lovely vales will be populated by beings almost human.

From Sydney he set sail for Honolulu. His wife and family would follow with Smyth on the *Julia Ann* and meet him in San Francisco.

In a curious footnote to the Young Ireland story, the two former allies, Mitchel and Meagher, ended up on opposite sides in the American Civil War of 1861—Mitchel on the southern side, supporting slavery, and Meagher as Brigadier General of the Irish Brigade on the Union side. In fact, all three of Mitchel's sons fought in an action against Meagher's troops. Two were killed, and the third lost an arm.

Returning to Ireland in 1874, Mitchel was elected twice as MP for Tipperary. The Westminster Parliament ruled that as a convicted felon he could not take his seat, and he died shortly after his second election in 1875. His lifelong friend John Martin, now pardoned and back in Ireland himself, was overcome with grief and died only nine days later.

Horton
College

Ask anyone in Tasmania where the major
private schools are and they'll happily tell
you, depending on which end of the island
they come from, that they're either in
Launceston or Hobart. Very few will be able
to tell you that just south of Ross on the
Midlands Highway there was once a large
college and boarding school for boys.

Horton College was set up by the former merchant
seaman Captain Samuel Horton of 'Somercotes'—a
house which still stands. As you travel north,
'Somercotes' is on your right, while the site of the now-demolished college is on the other side of the road. The farm that occupies the same site
is called 'Horton'. It was a Wesleyan college, Captain Horton being the
cousin of one of the founders of the Wesleyan church in Tasmania.

It had long been agreed that the new colony needed a college, but there
the agreement ended. None of the churches was prepared to admit that a
proper education could be had at a college run by any of the others, so the
Wesleyan community had no real choice other than to set up its own. The
foundation stone was laid in 1852, but as construction coincided with the

Victorian gold rush, there was a shortage of both labour and materials until the gold and the enthusiasm petered out. It was 1855 before the first student enrolled—the son of the first college President, Mr Manton. The prospectus differs little in its optimism and enthusiasm from those of 20th- and 21st-century colleges.

The college is situated on the Main Line of the Railway between Launceston and Hobart: in one of the most pleasant and healthy localities of Tasmania. The school-room, class-rooms, and dormitories are lofty, spacious and well ventilated; and each boy has a separate bed. There is a good and well selected Library. The playground is large, and a great extent of surrounding country is open for excursions. The river Macquarie, within a short distance, affords a safe and convenient bathing-place, the pupils enjoy this special advantage also, that they are altogether removed from the distractions of town life, and are thus enabled to give undivided attention to their studies. The course of study embraces all the branches of a thorough English Education, with Latin, Greek, French, Italian and Mathematics. In the higher forms the boys are prepared for the various Examinations under the Council of Education, and for Matriculation at the Universities...

Terms

Boarders under 15 years of age	£ 50 0 0	per annum
Boarders over 15 years of age	£ 60 0 0	per annum
Washing	£ 4 4 0	per annum
Medical attendance	£ 1 1 0	per annum
Music	£ 8 8 0	per annum
Drawing	£ 6 0 0	per annum
Drill	£ 11 0 0	per annum
Use of piano	£ 2 2 0	per annum

The vacations are seven weeks at midsummer and five weeks at midwinter. There are no holidays at Easter or Michaelmas...

List of articles required by each boarder
2 pairs sheets, 4 pillow cases, 6 towels, and a fork and spoon. Instead of the above a payment of £2 may be made at entrance. 3 suits of clothes, 1 overcoat, 6 shirts, 3 night shirts, 6 pairs socks, 8 pocket handkerchiefs, 3 pairs boots, 1 pair slippers, 1 brush and comb, 1

small tooth comb, 1 clothes brush, 1 tooth brush, 1 nail brush, 1 sponge and bag. Each article should be distinctly marked, and a list attached to the lid of the trunk.

Enrolments grew, as did the buildings, for about 40 years, until the college started to lose money due to a combination of economics and its location between two population centres (which amounts to economics). It had to close, and the buildings were given to Captain Horton's heir Mr Riggall on condition that he paid the debts of £250. His son lived in the residential part until he demolished it in 1917 and sold the materials. Some of the materials were used to build the present 'Horton' homestead, which is now also headed towards dereliction.

You can still hear the bell that summoned the Horton College students to meals, prayers and classes if you go to the Hutchins School in Hobart, where it now lives.

Horton College had a distinguished academic career, with many scholarships being won and many professional men being created. But like any boys' school it had its moments.

One was recorded in *The Mercury* in 1889, and was titled 'Eagle nesting at Horton College.' 'Eagle nesting' here refers not to the activity of the birds, but to the more human activity of stealing eggs from the nest. 'Hortonians have at all times been noted for their climbing propensities', the article said, but this one had surpassed himself by climbing a tree nearly 5 metres thick, and without limbs for the first 25 metres, so that he could get at the nest over 35 metres above the ground.

In an article for the Royal Society of Tasmania, E.R. Pretyman said 'it is probable that only two boys left their impressions of the school in print'…and goes on to quote a dull account of a day at the school by one of them.

A much more lively impression of the school was left by one of its less distinguished pupils, of whom the President Mr Quick wrote in 1862:

MY DEAR SIR,
I enclose two documents in Sunny's writing. They show,—(1.) What an evil influence he is exerting in the School. (2.) How he spends his valuable time. (3.) How impossible it is for him to attain any valuable object. They are, I assure you, but a specimen of his daily and hourly conduct. You cannot wish me to take him back next 'half'. More in grief than in anger I write that I will not have him in this School again. Indeed, I have told him that only an ample apology

will induce me to keep him here after tomorrow.
I am, My dear Sir,
Yours truly,
(Signed) W.A. QUICK.

The 'documents' were a rebellious note to the boy's brother, and a 20-stanza poem on the shortcomings of the college in general and 'Monsieur Nye' in particular. Two short samples from the poem:

A pretty little phiz he had,
A mouth that aught could grapple,
But in his gozzle sure there was
A thing called Adam's apple...

But soon behold him strut about,
And give his orders many,
At most of which we laughed full well,
And heeded few, if any.

What luxury it would be today, over a century later, to have enough writers of this calibre in a school to be able to expel one!

How to get there

The main front doorway of Horton College still stands, among the pine trees about 100 metres past the entrance to the 'Horton' property, which is on the western side of the Midland Highway a few hundred metres north of the turnoff to Mona Vale. This is private property and unfortunately the grandeur of the doorway is not quite visible from the road. In its shape, its size and its lonely location it calls to mind Shelley's *Ozymandias*, which was possibly studied at the school:

I met a traveller from an antique land,
Who said: two vast and trunkless legs of stone
Stand in the desert.
...My name is Ozymandias, king of kings:
Look on my works, ye mighty, and despair!

(Ironically, Oxford University did think it had enough writers of Shelley's calibre to expel him. He was sent down for writing a pamphlet called *The Necessity of Atheism*.)

The man who shrank the world

On the northern outskirts of Campbell Town,
in the Midlands, you'll see a sign pointing to
the Harold Gatty memorial. The memorial itself
is in the form of a globe of the world, with a
tiny aeroplane flying over the top. If you're an
aviation buff you may recognise the plane as
a Lockheed Vega, but then if you're an aviation
buff you don't need to be told
who Harold Gatty was.

J ust in case, in 1931 he and Wiley Post were the first to
fly around the world in an aeroplane.

The only reason the memorial is in Campbell Town,
incidentally, is that he was born there in 1903; which
seems fair enough until you realise that the following year his family
moved to Zeehan when his father, a schoolteacher, was transferred there.
Harold went to school in Zeehan and eventually won a bursary to St

Virgil's College in Hobart. From there he went to the Royal Australian Naval College in New South Wales.

After a number of years in the Merchant Navy, Gatty emigrated to the USA with his wife and son. He was interested in aviation, and was well aware that the techniques of marine navigation were inadequate for aerial navigation, so he worked on developing a new method. In fact he collaborated with Lieutenant–Commander P.V.H. Weems to produce what became known as the Weems system of air navigation.

Gatty set up a navigation school in Los Angeles, where one of his students was Mrs Charles Lindbergh. His collaboration with Weems on a book about aerial navigation was one of the events that brought him to the attention of the one-eyed flying genius, Wiley Post.

The other event was much more spectacular. In 1930, Gatty, navigating for the Canadian flyer Harold Bromley, tried to be the first to fly across the Pacific Ocean from Japan to America—12½ hours out over the ocean, a combination of mechanical trouble and thick fog forced the pair to turn back. Flying blind, Bromley and Gatty relied on dead reckoning alone to get themselves back to the same Japanese beach they had left from.

This safe landfall after 21 hours of flying blind was an astonishing feat of navigation, and it impressed Wiley Post so much that he contacted Gatty to chart a course for him in the coming Los Angeles to Chicago 'Derby' air race. When he won (flying, he said, for the first time ever on an accurately charted course), Post was impressed. When Art Goebel, the second flyer home, declared that he had also been helped by Gatty, Post was convinced. He approached Gatty immediately about an attempt to break the round-the-world record then held by the Graf Zeppelin airship— 21 days, 7 hours, 34 minutes.

Their aircraft, Winnie Mae, was a six-seat Lockheed Vega, modified by Post, with a supercharged 510-hp Pratt & Whitney Wasp engine and lots of extra fuel tanks. Gatty sat in the rear, in the passenger compartment, from where he could talk to Post through a speaking tube. Gatty's seat was not bolted down; this was so that he could move forward or back according to Post's directions to change the trim of the plane for landing and taking off. As Gatty was not a big man (just 1.6 metres tall and lightly built), this is an indication of the delicate balancing act they were performing with the fuel crammed into the plane.

As part of his meticulous preparation for the flight, Gatty invented an ingenious instrument that would measure drift and speed over anything that could be seen on the ground, provided the exact altitude was known. This has been described as the forerunner of the automatic pilot.

Despite getting bogged in mud twice (in Siberia and Canada), they flew into New York from the opposite direction just eight days after they had left—a feat described in detail in their book, *Around the World in Eight Days: The Flight of the Winnie Mae.*

Gatty went on to write two further books on navigation—one being *The Raft Book*, issued to US servicemen in World War II in case they were cast adrift at sea. The name is a misnomer—it's actually a kit in a cardboard sleeve, which promises, 'This book will tell you how to find your way to land—without instruments and without previous experience in navigation.' This beautiful little kit, which was published in 1943, contains the turquoise *Raft Book* itself (19.5 cm x 14 cm), with a silver wandering albatross and star motif embossed on the cover; the Gatty star chart; a set of tables and instructions about position finding; and a metre-long folded tape showing a Greenwich date and hour scale. The book details how to navigate to land using some simple charts and instruments (stick, string and a watch) and by using all the senses—observing the stars, birds, marine life, smells, sounds, the sky, cloud formations, wind, waves and swells, currents and sea colour.

Gatty enlarged on this theme in his final book, *Nature is your Guide*—an explanation of how some people, such as Polynesian sailors, can navigate and find their way around with such amazing accuracy just by using their senses (one of which, he assures us, is not the sense of direction.)

After his flight with Wiley Post, he became a celebrity in America, winning the DFC and eventually being placed in charge of Air Navigation, Research and Training for the US Army Air Corps. In World War II, the now Colonel Gatty was McArthur's Director of Air Transport for the Allied Air forces.

When he left the services, Gatty went to live in Fiji, where he bought his own island, started Fijian Airways (later Air Pacific) and ran a coconut plantation. He is credited with opening the air routes from America to Asia, Australia and New Zealand.

Harold Gatty died in Suva in 1957, leaving the world a far smaller place than it was at the time of his birth in 1903.

Hospital in the bush

In Campbell Town's Valentine Park
picnic ground, a stone cairn commemorates
a 600-bed hospital that was built just up
the road, at 'Merton Vale',
during World War II.

I t had been decided in 1939 that Tasmania needed a military hospital. The 111th Australian General Hospital therefore came into being— first at Brighton, then at the Royal Hobart Hospital, and then, in 1942, at Campbell Town. While the hospital was being built (at a total cost of £1500!), temporary accommodation for patients and staff was found in a cottage and hall in the town. It took eight months for the hospital to be built on 17.5 hectares at 'Merton Vale', mostly of unlined vertical-board huts. Over the next 12 months, before the hospital was lined, patients and staff were often subjected to extreme cold. It was a full year after the move to Campbell Town before the hospital was ready for its official opening by the Governor of Tasmania, Sir Ernest Clark.

Curiously for a military hospital, the 111th A.G.H. was at its busiest after the war was over. This was because all the wounded and sick Tasmanians came home at the end of hostilities, and the numbers were further swelled by ex-Prisoners of War who still needed treatment.

The hospital site closed down in 1946 after the last of its estimated 50 000 patients had been transferred to other hospitals either in Tasmania or on the mainland.

A Tasmanian
icon

Ask any Tasmanian about Marjorie Bligh,
and you're likely to be told that she's the
lady who can make *anything* out of supermarket
bags; or the lady who used to win everything
at the Campbell Town show; or the lady who
used to live in 'Climar' —'that house with
the funny fence' in Campbell Town.

T he fence in question, clearly visible from the main road, is made of wrought iron and has the notes of the first verse of *Melody of Love* wrought cunningly into it. This was her favourite song at the time the house was built. It was designed by the lady herself, took four years to build, and was so unusual at the time (1955) that people from far and near stopped and took pictures. Marjorie was happy to give tours and have people sign the visitors' book. It is still an unusual house even today, with its curved walls and curved glass frontage, sandblasted 'in a pleasing design'.

These days she lives in Devonport, at 163 Madden Street, in a house distinguished by another 'funny fence'. This fence is superbly made, including custom-made gates, and appears to be designed to keep a miniature poodle inside; it's about 300 millimetres high and the gates are best negotiated by stepping over them. (If you are bold enough to step beyond the first mat with its 'Welcome' message, onto the second with 'No Smoking', and ring the doorbell, you'll hear *Fur Elise* booming out—a lengthy version that is presumably designed to entertain the visitor and the rest of the street while the lady of the house puts away her current craft project.)

Marjorie Bligh has achieved icon status in Tasmania, with a string of self-published books to her credit. These include:

Marjorie Bligh's Homely Hints on Everything (which is exactly what it says)

Marjorie Bligh's A to Z Book on Gardening (ditto)

At Home with Marjorie Bligh (again, a fair description of the content)

Crafts: Old, New, Recycled (in which amazing and unlikely things are made from other things that most of us usually throw away)

Tasmania and Beyond (an account of some of her travels)

Life is for Living: The Heartaches and Happiness of Marjorie Bligh with Snippets of Travel, Wisdom and History (a combined autobiography and philosophy, drawn presumably from her diaries, and with some details of a home life that has at times been less than idyllic)

The Formation and History of the Devonport Branch (of the Country Women's Association).

If you've never read one of Marjorie Bligh's books, you owe it to yourself to dip into one. They are like an old-fashioned shop—filled with a huge variety of material, the old mixed with the new, the useful mixed with the less so, and the whole thing looking as if a good tidy-up would take away its reason for being.

Certainly, the reader is always aware of the author's opinion on any subject that may come up in the numerous digressions along the way. Where she feels that a wider lesson about life can be learnt, an italicised aphorism is sure to follow the story.

Behind all the homespun wisdom and extraneous information, however, there is a lot of genuinely useful and equally homespun information.

Radioactive
Rossarden

Any Tasmanian will happily tell you
how rich in minerals our State is, but
very few will be able to tell you
that we have uranium here.

T he only finds so far thought worthy of development have
been in the Fingal Valley.

The first discovery of rich minerals was in 1955, at the old Royal George Tin Mine, near Avoca. The green crystals of copper uranite, or torbernite, were found and a reward was paid to their finder.

Later, a company called Tasmanian United Uranium extracted some black uranium–bearing material, presumably pitchblende, from a point on Storys Creek, 3 kilometres downstream from Rossarden. None of it was sold, but it was prepared for sale and there was a commercial quantity of it. One wonders where it is now.

Deddington
Chapel

If you're a local you may have heard
people talking about 'Upper Blessington'
in the same way as 'The Back of Bourke'
or 'The Black Stump', as a synonym for
a long way off the beaten track.

T he village of Deddington is distinguished by being
on the way to Blessington and Upper Blessington;
there its significance would end, if it were not for
the little chapel by the roadside. It is described in the Tasmanian Heritage
Register as 'a simple Georgian chapel of painted brick with gabled roof
and close eaves.'

This chapel was designed by a man who is recognised as one of the greatest landscape artists of the 19th century, and the man who first painted the Australian landscape as it actually appeared—John Glover. It is not surprising that he designed the chapel, since he lived just up the road from it.

Glover, a successful painter, and coming from 'old money', was already in his sixties and well off when he followed his two grown-up sons to Van Diemen's Land in 1831. After setting up two farms in the south and appointing managers to run them, he was granted about 1000 hectares along the Nile River, outside Deddington. He named his new two-storey stone house 'Patterdale', after a village in England's Lake District, and soon built up his holding to about 3000 hectares.

A measure of his success as a painter is that when he arrived here and applied for a land grant he was able to show that he had brought £7000 with him, had assets worth over £50,000, and expected his income from painting alone to be £1000 a year. (In 1835 he sent to England no less than 68 paintings of Tasmanian scenes, so his estimate was apparently accurate.)

Glover was obviously a man of considerable energy, despite having two club feet. At the age of 65, he and his neighbour John Batman (the captor of Matthew Brady) were in the party of the first white people to reach the 1500-metre summit of Ben Lomond.

After a long and distinguished career as an artist and gentleman farmer, Glover died in 1849, aged 82, and was buried beside the little chapel he had designed—his grave was rediscovered and the stone engraved early in the 20th century.

There has been considerable speculation about what makes a wealthy and popular artist uproot his family and go to live on the other side of the world. Certainly the fact that his sons went first was an influence. There is no need to speculate about why he stayed (albeit with regular trips back to England)—he liked it here. His son wrote, 'This climate is certainly most salutary, and as to health, we all, thank God, enjoy it...'

An intriguing footnote is that while still living in England Glover was awarded a gold medal by King Louis XVIII of France for his painting *The Bay of Naples*. Before he could receive the medal, however, Napoleon escaped from Elba and marched on Paris, forcing both Louis XVIII and Glover to flee. Glover eventually received his medal in England as a gift from Napoleon. The medal ended up on loan to the Queen Victoria Museum and Art Gallery in Launceston, but was stolen from there in 1904. Where it is now, and whether it has been melted down, is very much a part of secret Tasmania.

How to get there

Turn onto the C420, close to Nile. Deddington
is 9 kilometres down the road.

State Secrets

Man's best friend...
and worst enemy

Until the late 1970s, Tasmania was thought of (with some cause) as the Hydatids capital of the world. Thanks to some far-sighted research, careful planning and hard work, this ghastly disease has now been virtually eradicated from the State.

Considering the resources that the disease employs, it is an incredible achievement that a generation is now growing up who have never seen or heard of it.

Until the late 1960s it was common practice on Tasmanian farms to kill sheep for food and then feed the household and farm dogs on the offal. It was also a lethal practice, because it invited a particularly hideous and deadly parasite into the household.

The parasite in question is the *echinococcus granulosis* worm, also known as the hydatid tapeworm. Its life cycle in the wild typically involves a herbivore (say, a sheep) and a carnivore (a dog). It lives in the carnivore's gut in its adult stage. It is a very small worm (5–7 millimetres long), with a relatively slow rate of reproduction (about 50 eggs a day), and the infestation is typically a very large one, usually thousands of worms. When the eggs are excreted, the grass is contaminated, the herbivore eats it and the larval cycle starts. The larvae live a long time, and are slow to develop. But when they do develop, they burrow into the vital organs and form cysts. These cysts produce further larvae by the hundreds of thousands, and when the animal dies of the cysts, carnivores eat them and the cycle begins again.

The part played by people in all this is purely incidental, and comes from their relationship with the sheep and the dog. When we handle a dog that is infected with hydatid worms, we can quite easily eat the tiny eggs unless we are very careful about hygiene. Children typically are not, so they are the ones most likely to be infected. The results for us are the same as they are for the sheep—the cysts grow over a long time, often becoming enormous and painful, and ultimately kill the host unless major surgery is carried out. The biggest cyst ever found in a human being (in Africa) was a 50-litre one—as big as ten wine casks. Although the cysts do not affect the organs themselves, they do invade their territory, and the effect and pain of a large cyst pressing on a vital organ can be imagined. They can also kill their host if they burst accidentally.

So how was this awful disease eradicated? Officers of the Department of Agriculture, led by G.K. Meldrum, realised in the 1960s that there were two problems—tracking and treating parasite infections in dogs and sheep, and educating owners about how to avoid re-infestation.

'Hydatids testing strips' were set up all over the State, and mobile test stations went out to these sites to carry out testing of dogs for hydatids. The test strips were fenced-off strips of land by the roadside, marked with danger signs and white posts, with pegs for tying up dogs. If the testing officers were working, an aluminium caravan could be seen on the strip.

In a 20-year period between 1965 and 1985 the number of infected dogs fell from 881 (12% of tested animals!) to zero. Over the same period, the percentages of infected sheep fell in a similar way. Human infestations fell from 19 to two (both over 50 years old, and therefore possibly infected years before).

Although there is a drug that is capable of killing the hydatid tapeworm in dogs (and that has been used to control infected dogs), the most important measure in beating the disease was not the drug, but the good sense of most Tasmanian farmers in learning not to feed offal to their dogs and disposing quickly of sheep carcasses. (Unfortunately, and paradoxically, the fact that an effective drug is now available over the counter means that some rural dog owners may get careless again—so the disease may never be completely eradicated.)

Things that can hurt you

We really should put 'your car' at the
top of this list, as you're far more likely to
be hurt in a traffic accident than by any of the
animals and fish listed below. Indeed, even
among our list of 'dangerous species',
there are a few surprises.

For example, the most dangerous animal in Tasmania in terms of deaths caused is probably the honey bee. You're fairly safe up in the air, unless you are attacked by an eagle, but on land and in the sea there are quite a few things that can hurt or kill you.

Any snake in Tasmania should be left alone. There are three species—tiger snakes, copperheads and whitelipped (whip) snakes—and they're all venomous. Take particular care on summer evenings and in long grass.

Spiders we have referred to elsewhere, but three that are worthy of mention are the redback, the white-tipped spider and the black house spider. Redbacks (which have a red 'racing stripe' on their backs) live in shady spots like old sheds, and their bite hurts but is unlikely to kill.

The white-tipped spider is a small, cigar-shaped arachnid with a white tail tip, and you're quite likely to find it under a pile of clothes on the floor. Its bite can cause nasty ulcers. The black house spider is very common on the corners of windows, and its bite is very painful but not especially dangerous. However it is fairly sizeable and visible, so it can be avoided. All spiders have fangs, most can bite, and venomous or not, their diet of flies and the like is not the sort of thing you want infecting your bloodstream. So even the relatively harmless ones like huntsmen should not be handled.

Also under the heading of creepy-crawlies are scorpions. The further south scorpions go, the less nasty they are—and Tasmania is about as far south as they get. You're most likely to find them in a load of firewood, and you're most likely to get stung if you interfere with them.

Other guests you may find in a load of wood are bull ants and jack-jumpers. Both these ants are quite sizeable, and both can give you a very painful sting with their tail. This may be complicated by an allergy to the sting on your part. (People who build up an allergy find that each sting has a progressively worse effect on them; they may even die.)

The European honey bee is generally too busy to be bothered with stinging people, but if provoked it will sting, and die in doing so. Here again, you (or someone else) may have developed a lethal allergy, so bees should be left alone.

The European wasp is a very different kettle of venom. It's a nasty, aggressive creature, and it tends to fight fire with fire. If you swat at it and miss, it will certainly have a go at you, stinging repeatedly. Unfortunately these pests are not killed by the cold in the Tasmanian winter, which means that here their nests can be several metres across and have millions of wasps in them. One is dangerous; millions don't bear thinking about.

The most dangerous thing you're likely to find in a river is, incredibly, the platypus. If you are ever foolhardy enough to pick up a male platypus, you'll discover, just after he clamps his rear legs together around your arm, that he has spines inside his rear legs that can inject poison. Although it is not lethal, this is quite fantastically painful, and is an excellent reason for looking and not touching.

Tasmanian sea life has a good selection of the don't-touch, the poisonous, the venomous and the frankly predatory. The blue-ringed octopus, for example, is a very small (only about 12 centimetres across), beautifully coloured octopus that is commonly found in rock pools at the low tide mark. Admire its colours by all means, but if its rings turn a shimmering blue it is ready to bite, and its poison has a potentially deadly paralysing effect. Then there is the Portuguese Man-of-War—which is a bit of a misnomer, because it's more of an armada of jellyfish sailing together than a single ship of the line. Under the water, when hunting, it trails tentacles up to 10 metres long, which can give a lot of very painful stings.

Another stinger is the stingray. If you tread on one of these it will show its displeasure by driving a sting into you forcefully with its tail. Not only is this extraordinarily unpleasant, its effects can last a long time. You won't die unless it gets you in the heart, but you may consider dying as pain relief.

Toadfish and puffer fish will get their revenge on you if you eat them. Their flesh is very poisonous. However, they're covered in spines and have a set of teeth like piranhas, so you should be able to resist the urge to fry them up. Speaking of spines, the humble flathead probably injures more fishermen every year than any other fish, and the scorpionfish can give you an even nastier poke if you're silly enough to touch its formidable armoury.

Sharks can also be found in Tasmanian waters. The good news is that only a few of them (the bronze whaler, the tiger shark and the great white shark) are known to attack people. The bad news is that the great white likes the cool water here, and has been blamed for several attacks. You are, however, more likely to be knocked down by a bus on the way to the beach than to meet or be attacked by a shark—so look carefully before you step into the road. In the sea, don't swim in poor light, don't swim alone and leave seal colonies alone. (A seal colony at St Albans Bay was the scene of Tasmania's most tragic attack, in 1993, when mother of five, Therese Cartwright, was killed by a great white shark while diving.)

There have been three fatal shark attacks in Tasmania in the last 30 years, but there have been twice as many close encounters and unfinished attacks. Even in a boat you may not be safe, as a family fishing for squid at Kingston in 1998 found out when a 3-metre thresher shark deliberately jumped into their boat. They managed to kill it with the boat anchor, but not before it had given them a nasty scare.

In a suburban garden there are likely to be a number of things that can poison you if you eat them. Since it's difficult to eat things accidentally (unlike treading on a snake or a stingray), it's fairly easy for an adult to avoid poisoning. Just make sure you know what you're eating, and that it's safe to eat. And keep an eye on the kids. Rhubarb, for example, is okay, but rhubarb leaves are not. Cotoneaster berries look enticing but are poisonous. Some mushrooms are delicious; some are lethal. (There are even some that are both delicious and lethal, as the Emperor Claudius could tell you if he hadn't eaten a plate of them.)

Dunnies
both old
and new

The English actor Sir Bernard Miles
once narrated and starred in a short pseudo-
documentary film, set presumably in the
19th century, in which he claimed to be
'yer county champion privy builder'.

I n his bucolic commentary he said that the criteria for success in a privy (the renowned Australian outhouse) were the smoothness of the wood, the circularity of the hole or holes and the degree of creativity applied to the light-hole in the door. He also classified privies by size, as one-, two-, three- and even four-holers. He didn't mention vandalism, graffiti or syringes, but he did give one piece of advice that still applies to the long-drop dunny—'when you dig 'er, take my advice and dig 'er deep. 'Cos you don't want to have to move 'er.'

In Tasmania you can of course still find long-drop one-holers, mostly in remote camping areas. (Our teenage son found one at Twilight Tarn that "adn't been dug deep enough', or had been filled more than quickly enough; this, among other things, was impressed on him when he hurled in a large rock and the displaced contents rushed up to meet him.)

Some of these bush dunnies enjoy spectacular views, if you leave the door open. Perhaps the best view of all is enjoyed by the one at Lake Tahune, near Frenchmans Cap.

Little did Sir Bernard's character in the film know that the privy of the future would be a temple of technology. You'll find a good example of this in the 'Exeloo' in Launceston's Paterson Street Car Park behind Birchalls. The door of this polygonal Tardis-like structure is open when you walk up to it. Classical music starts when you use one of the buttons inside to close the door. Wherever you look inside, technology has been used in an attempt to defeat vandals—the stainless steel electric one-sheet toilet roll dispenser, the stainless steel soap dispenser, the built-in hand-drier... Mind you, vandals are nothing if not persistent—someone has tried to set fire to the door buttons, with a cavalier disregard for how he was going to get out if he succeeded. (No doubt the feminists will forgive us this gender assumption—an unwarranted one, given that these toilets of the future are unisex ones.) Strangely enough, the scientific accomplishment stops short of the plumbing. In both toilets of this type that we have used (there's another at Wentworth Park, in the Hobart suburb of Howrah), the water tap comes on so violently that it soaks both client and floor.

Elsewhere in the State, the public dunnies are occasionally designed to blend with the architecture of the area (not necessarily a desirable feature, given the degree of urgency sometimes involved in looking for them). Harrington Street in Hobart has an elderly stone edifice, built ominously over the Hobart Rivulet. Bothwell has splendid sandstone facilities, while Dunalley has a Nissen hut-like semicylinder squatting by the canal bank.

And if you're ever driving around Longford searching for the remains of the racetrack, take the turnoff to Mill Dam—a weir which is an old-fashioned swimming and picnic area. It has quaint Gents' and Ladies' dressing sheds made from concrete tanks, and toilets apparently made from half tanks.

Sir Bernard would be impressed with 21st century privies, despite the demise of his hallowed four-holer.

How to get there

Thanks to an initiative by the Federal Government, every toilet in Australia is now marked on a map! So if you're looking for any Tasmanian dunny, go to www.toiletmap.gov.au.

'Look before you buzz. Who or what is in the open aisle?'

Although the State Library of Tasmania's headquarters is a highly visible building on the corner of Murray and Bathurst streets in Hobart, it has a less visible side in its various heritage collections.

There are three of these—the Allport Library and Museum of Fine Arts, the W.L. Crowther Collection and the Tasmaniana Library.

The Allport Library and Museum of Fine Arts is on the ground floor of the library building; and while there is nothing secret about it, it would be very easy to remain unaware of its existence unless you're a frequent user of the library's newspaper collection. In the back corner of the hall that houses the newspapers you'll see an open portal, which leads off into a remarkable area where a 19th-century gentleman's house has been recreated in separate rooms, each laden with its own treasures. There is a bedroom, a dining room, a number of drawing rooms and games rooms (Mr Allport appears to have been keen on board and card games) and of course a library. It's not, perhaps, exactly the kind of thing you would expect to find in a public library; but it's there and it's definitely worth seeing if only for the craftsmanship of the furniture.

A couple of floors up, and accessible via the Reference Library, is the Tasmaniana Collection and the W.L. Crowther Collection. The Crowther Collection is a huge array of books, publications, photographs, medals and memorabilia relating not only to Tasmania but to the rest of Australia and the world. It's named after a member of the very distinguished Crowther family of doctors, collectors, politicians and amateur anthropologists. Various members of the family scowl down from portraits on the walls.

The Tasmaniana Library lives in the same quarters as the Crowther Collection. The collection that forms the backbone of the Tasmaniana Library was donated by William Walker, a Hobart book collector, in 1924. After his death his widow made a further donation in 1933. The Library's function today is to gather every significant publication originating in or relating to Tasmania, regardless of where in the world it is published.

It is the job of Tony Marshall, Senior Librarian of the Heritage Collections, to make sure that this keeps happening, and to make sure that the resulting collection is accessible to the public. Wherever he goes—to book dealers, antique shops, or auctions—his eye is watching for things the library may want. When we talked to him he had just visited an antique shop in Evandale and had come away with several new treasures—a number of old postcards and a 1940s plan of the 'Joyce's Estate' subdivision, near the paper mill at Burnie.

Tony is quick to point out, however, that 'heritage' doesn't necessarily mean 'historical'. In other words, things do not have to be old to be in a heritage collection. They just have to have enough significance to be worth preserving as a part of future history. On the shelves, accessible but not generally visible, there are CDs, videos, audio tapes, medals, banners, advertisements, table napkins, maps, brochures and many other types of publication, including, of course, books.

There's no such thing as a representative sample of a collection so eclectic, but some of the curios we saw are listed below:

- A facsimile edition of Matthew Flinders' *A Voyage to Terra Australis* (see page 68) is one of the largest items in the collection, and certainly comes in the largest container. Some of the smallest are the miniature editions of newspapers brought out to celebrate important events, or the tiny handbook *The Medical Telephone*, put out by the Homoeopathic Pharmacy (today known as Gould's).

- The only known copy of Robert Marsh's *Seven Years of My Life or Narrative of A Patriot Exile*—a story published in 1847 about a group of Canadian patriots who were transported to Van Diemen's Land. This unique book was bought at auction by the State Library. Like about 300 other items, it lives in its own little box as part of a program of protection for things that are rare or delicate. For the last three years these boxes, works of art in their own right, have been produced by a specialist box-maker.

- Less rare but still important is the battered first edition three-volume *Quintus Servinton* by Henry Savery, the first novel published in Australia. This book will be left unrestored, because there are other copies available, and because Tony describes himself as 'a great believer in historical dirt'.

- A playbill, printed on silk, from the Royal Victoria Theatre (now the Theatre Royal) is an example of the theatrical ephemera that find their way into the collection. In this case a telephone call from an itinerant gentleman in Queensland heralded his arrival some months later with two of these 1840s playbills, wrapped in tea towels and preserved in exquisitely perfect condition, which he wanted to sell.

- A true survivor is a program, in the form of a tissue paper table napkin, from an 1899 performance of *The Mikado*. Theatre programs, unlike reviews, always say who performed what, which makes them particularly important as heritage pieces. Cheek-by-jowl with this are a large banner, windcheater, poster and even a fridge magnet from a recent Tasmanian production of *Les Misérables*.

- An early (and very good) example of colour printing by *The Mercury* is a handbill advertising a trip on the ferry *Nubeena* to go out and meet the *Harlech Castle* bringing the troops back from the Boer War.

- *Aurora Australis* is a book that was printed in 1908 at the headquarters of the British Antarctic Expedition in Antarctica. Only about 100 copies were printed—the miracle being that they could get a printing press to work at all in the Antarctic—and at last count, 60 of these had been tracked down. Beautifully produced, the book is bound in wood made from the containers they had with them; the one in the Tasmaniana collection still has 'Julienne Soup' stencilled on the inside back cover, and was presented to Captain John King Davis, master of the Antarctic vessel *Nimrod*, by the artist and printers. The book was presented to the collection by Captain Davis, and is thought to be worth about $35,000.

- Apple labels, at the time they were produced, were just something stuck on the end of a crate; and while some were beautiful in their own right, no-one would have viewed them (or the apple industry) as an endangered species. Today the Tasmaniana Library is still acquiring them, to add to the present large collection.

When you make a request for any of these things from the catalogue, they are fetched by one of the librarians from 'stack'—the area where the collection lives. This is a well-lit area filled with electrically operated compactus shelving that buzzes loudly when you press a button to move it. A notice on the wall warns, 'Look before you buzz. Who or what is in the open aisle?' Librarians do not view crush injuries as being in the line of duty.

There are seven staff members (7.2 to be exact) looking after the three heritage collections, and they are kept busy by a stream of inquiries from a wide variety of users. About twenty people a day walk through the doors of the Tasmaniana Library and Crowther Collection, and they include academics, professional researchers, graphic designers, consultants, students of all ages, writers, and a host of other people with pet projects to pursue. Genealogical research (the family tree) is a common reason for people to come in, but they don't always find what they're looking for.

'We're the place to put leaves on the family tree, if you like—to find out what their ancestors actually did, rather than just who they were,' says Tony. 'But we can certainly direct them to other places that are more likely to have what they want.'

The people who arrive in the library and ask for a book or item in the flesh are just a part of the whole body of users. Others write, phone, fax, or email their queries. The emailers are growing in number, as is the Tasmaniana collection's interest in digital information. In the collection you will now even find web sites; and as new technologies become available the range of media and of items in the collection will no doubt increase. The heritage collections have their own web pages, too, on the State Library of Tasmania's web site.

Is there a particular type of inquiry that heritage librarians grow tired of hearing? He laughs. 'Well, we do get a bit tired of explaining the photocopying rules' (nothing from before 1900 may be photocopied), 'and we sometimes get people researching family trees who expect us to have exactly the same level of interest in their project as they have themselves. But I think that happens to all librarians'.

Tasmanian
tiger—
is it or
isn't it?

The history books will tell you that the
last male 'Tasmanian tiger' or thylacine
died in captivity in Beaumaris Zoo, Hobart,
in 1936. But a large number of people, many
with a full complement of marbles, will tell
you that they have seen them in
the bush since then.

I ndeed, it would be arrogant and gullible of us to assume that the last one living happened to be in captivity, but then our relationship with the animal has always been driven by arrogance and gullibility. Greed, too, got its chance when the thylacine began to kill sheep, the easiest prey imaginable. It never seems to have occurred to us that for millennia before we arrived, the thylacine had got along perfectly well without eating a single sheep. We never asked why in the 19th century it would suddenly change its dietary habits and live apparently exclusively on mutton, or even, as some enthusiastic persecutors suggested, on blood alone. Some properties employed 'tiger men' specifically to kill thylacines; some adopted more careful shep-herding tactics, which were very successful in preventing losses of all kinds.

Then, as now, the main cause of sheep losses was theft. Then, as now, devils often ate carcasses overnight, making it impossible to tell what had killed the sheep. Then, as now, public figures told lies for personal gain. One parliamentarian said that thylacines were killing 50 000 sheep a year on the East Coast in 1886. As tiger-tracker Dr Eric Guiler points out, this was half the total sheep population of the coast—enough to bankrupt every grazier living there. Yet this ludicrous figure was believed, to the extent that a bounty of £1 was placed on the thylacine's head from 1887 onwards. This bounty was to be claimed 2184 times between 1888 and 1909.

Persecution by the white race was not the sole cause of the thylacine's demise; habitat alteration, competition from wild dogs, and disease may also have contributed. But what amounted to a dedicated campaign to hunt the animal to extinction is an inexcusable and unforgettable blot on the history of Tasmania. It was partially protected in 1930, and a government-sponsored expedition set out to search for it in the year of its final official demise. These measures demonstrate exactly how forward-looking were the governments who dealt with the thylacine.

The question that has been asked for many years is, 'Are they still out there?' There have been over 300 alleged sightings since the last one in captivity died, and over 100 of these are viewed as credible.

One authority on the animal told us some years ago that he thought it 'more likely than not'. However, he has since changed his opinion and regretfully conceded that they are now probably all gone. There have been many searches, some of them highly professional and well-equipped; there has even been a large financial reward offered by American yachtsman and media magnate Ted Turner; but no sign of the animal has emerged beyond footprints, possible dung and the reports of sightings by others.

In a State where a good sampling of the local wildlife is invariably avail-able for inspection on the roads every morning, it is curious, too, that no thylacine has been run over in the last 65 years.

One thing that seems certain, however, is that the last thylacine did not die in 1936. On very large and remote properties like 'Woolnorth' there seems to be good evidence, in the form of scats and footprints, that they were still around in the 1950s and 1960s. If there are still any alive, it is to be expected (and hoped) that this is where they are.

Two
heads...

Jibes about people having two heads are
common fare to anyone who admits to living
in Tasmania. Mostly we laugh them off, 'because
we're not really like that'. But where do the stories
of inbreeding and unfortunate offspring come
from? And do they have any basis in fact?

T hey do. But not the facts you might expect. There
are areas of Tasmania where it's generally believed
that inbreeding takes place. Typically they are rural
communities, where choice of partners is limited.

From places like these come yarns like the one about the bushman
whose father had been killed by a falling tree, and who brought him to the
local police station in a sack, having 'jointed him up with th'axe' because
he couldn't get all of him out from under the tree. And the family who
were visited by the health inspector and told that brothers' and sisters'
sleeping accommodation had to be kept separate—a feat that had been
achieved with a roll of barbed wire the next time the inspector called. (In
the versions I have heard, *all* the people had the same surname.)

But are these happenings (if true) attributable to anything other than
eccentricity? There is evidence to suggest that they are.

If you've read this far rather than slamming the book shut in disgust, you
probably believe that the type of community where this occurs is a poor
rural one, isolated in every way. While it's true that the (alleged) examples
above are taken from just such a community, there are other factors that
contribute to inbreeding. One of them, ironically, is wealth, in the form of
land. As large amounts of land were granted to small numbers of people in

the 19th century, there has been a tendency ever since for these land-owners to attempt to hold onto their heritage by ensuring that they married other landowners. There is only a finite amount of land in Tasmania, so the 'suitable' mates have at times been few and far between.

What are the effects of inbreeding? To put it simply, if a parent has a mutation, or a predisposition to a particular disease, part of that is passed on to the children. If the other parent has the same predisposition, there is a much higher probability of it being passed on to the children. If they in turn mate with people who are related to them, the problem compounds. It may not show right away; nor will it always show up; but it does not go away.

Another source of 'two-head' and similar stories might be the tendency towards goitre (an enlarged thyroid gland) and related illnesses that were once frequently found in Tasmania. Many parts of the State have iodine deficiencies in the soil and water, caused by it leaching away during the Ice Age, and these deficiencies (passed on to the food) have led to disease in families that have lived in the same area for a long time. Typical of these diseases are goitre and cretinism. The symptoms of cretinism are deform-ity, dwarfism and mental retardation. Because the symptoms tend to appear in the same families, who are all undergoing the same iodine deprivation, the assumption that they are hereditary is (although incorrect) quite reasonable. Some of the 'inbreeding' myths probably stem from exactly this problem and have nothing to do with inbreeding.

When it became apparent that Tasmania had an iodine deficiency, meas-ures were taken in 1950 to correct it. Schoolchildren and parents were issued with weekly dosages of potassium iodide 'goitre' tablets. While these worked if taken regularly, and there was a fall in goitre incidence, there were problems. Some parents were less than religious about handing them out, or stored them too long, and there was wide variation in the effi-ciency of schools in handing them out. It was therefore decided in 1965 that tablets wouldn't work, and iodated bread improvers became our main source of extra iodine for the next decade. Where do we get our extra iodine these days? Mostly from commercial milk, as the dairy industry uses it as a sanitising agent. The baking industry has now agreed to use iodised salt to counter a recent relapse into iodine deficiency, and iodine can also be taken in from yoghurt, milk, tinned salmon and sea fish.

On the one hand, it may be that the stories we have all heard of 'inbreeding' are in fact just ignorant interpretations of iodine deficiency symptoms. On the other hand, human beings are very complex creatures, so it may also be that the symptoms themselves have led to a higher inci-dence of inbreeding. The truth probably lies somewhere in the middle.

References

A visit from Hell
Wettenhall, R.L 1975, *Bushfire Disaster: An Australian Community in Crisis*, Angus and Robertson, Sydney.

In like Flynn
Flynn, Errol 1959, *My Wicked, Wicked Ways*, G.P. Putnam's Sons, New York.
Niven, David 1975, *Bring on the Empty Horses*, Hamilton, London.
Norman, Don 1981, *Errol Flynn: The Tasmanian Story*, W.N. Hurst and E.L. Metcalf, Hobart.

Friends Park
A Guide to Hobart's Historic Cemeteries and Burial Grounds, Hobart City Council, 2000.

Keen as...
Edwards, Jack 1982, *Out of the Blue: A History of Reckitt and Colman in Australia*, Reckitt and Colman, Artarmon.

Cornelian Bay and the boatsheds
Barraclough, Julian 1999, *Cornelian Bay Planning Study*, Hobart City Council.
Hobart Town Advertiser, 29.10.1850, 'Voracity of the Shark'.

The corpse in the fountain
Tasmanian Architect, January 1962

April Fools' Day revisited
City of Hobart Lord Mayor's Report, 1954–1956, Tasmania.

Walking Sullivans Cove
Sullivans Cove Development Authority 1988, *A Sullivans Cove Walk*, Tourism Tasmania, Hobart.

From drudgery to fudgery
Crooke, Robert 1958, *The Convict*, University of Tasmania Library.
Searle, Cathie 1998, 'Valley of the Shadow: The Story of the Cascades Female Factory', in *40° South*, Edition 10.

Rory's story
Thompson, Rory Jack 1993, *Mad Scientist*, Southern Holdings, Huonville.
Tennent, Shan 2001, *Deaths in Custody Inquest: Findings: Chris William Douglas, Thomas Patrick Holmes, Jack Newman, Laurence Colin Santos, Fabian Guy Long*, Tasmania Magistrates Court, Hobart.

The Conrad connection
Conrad, Peter 1988, *Down Home: Revisiting Tasmania*, Chatto and Windus, London.

Neil Davis, frontline cameraman
Bowden, Tim 1987, *One Crowded Hour: Neil Davis, Combat Cameraman, 1934–1985*, Angus & Robertson, Sydney.
Bradbury, David 1980, *Frontline*, ABC Television.

Tragedy at Trefoil Island
Wellington Times, 30 November 1895.
Pink, K. & Ebdon, A. 1988, *Beyond the Ramparts: A Bicentennial History of Circular Head*, Circular Head Bicentennial History Group.

Darwin Crater—the invisible impact
Fudali, R.F., & Ford, R.J. 1984, *Darwin Glass and Darwin Crater: A Progress Report*, Meteoritics, Arizona State University, Center for Meteorite Studies, USA.
Richardson, R.G. 1984, *Geophysical Surveys of the Darwin Crater, Unpublished report*.
Hills, Loftus 1915, *Darwin Glass: A New Variety of Tektites*, Tasmanian Mines Department, Hobart.

A modest genius
Flinders, Matthew 1800, *Observations on the Coasts of Van Diemen's Land, on Bass's Strait and its Islands and on part of the Coasts of New South Wales*; Review Publications, Sydney.
Flinders, Matthew 1989, *A Voyage to Terra Australis: Undertaken for the Purpose of Completing the Discovery of that Vast Country, and Prosecuted in the Years 1801, 1802 and 1803...*, Facsimile edition, South Australian Government Printer, South Australia.
Flinders, Matthew, Ed. Tim Flannery 2000, *Terra Australis: Matthew Flinders' Great Adventures in the Circumnavigation of Australia*, Text Publishing, Melbourne.

The Franklins' journey
Alexander, Alison 1999, *Obliged to Submit: Wives and Mistresses of Colonial Governors*, Montpelier Press, Hobart.
Burn, David 1842, Ed. George Mackaness 1955, *Narrative of the Overland Journey of Sir John and Lady Franklin and Party from Hobart Town to Macquarie Harbour*, D.S. Ford, Sydney.

The seizure of Rocky Cape
Wood, Barry 1993, *Two Cultures in Conflict: Rocky Cape National Park Dispute, 1991-1993* (Unpublished dissertation).

Sisters Beach
Irby, Kenneth 1972, *In the Beginning: Sisters Creek Beach, a Tasmanian Family Starts a Town*, Kenneth Irby, Sisters Creek Beach.

The mother of Cradle Mountain-Lake St Clair National Park
Schnackenberg, Sally 1995, *Kate Weindorfer: The Woman Behind the Man and the Mountain: A Biography of Kate Julia Weindorfer wife of Cradle Mountain Pioneer Gustav Weindorfer*, Regal Publications, Launceston.

Dorfer's death
Fred Smithies Collection, Archives Office of Tasmania
The amazing mazes of Tasmazia
Fisher, A. & Gerster, G. 1990, *The Art of the Maze,* Weidenfeld and Nicolson, London.
Yes, there is a Sawdust Bridge
Gardam, Faye 1996, *Sawdust, Sails and Sweat: A History of the River Don Settlement, North-West Coast, Tasmania,*
Richmond Printers, Devonport.
Big man, big heart
Foster, David and Edwards, R.F. 1998, *The Power of Two: The David Foster Story,* Random House, Sydney.
The dredge and the cruiser
Chamberlain, Brian 1993, *Tamar Mud and Ponrabbel,* Launceston.
Van der Vat, Dan 1983, *The Last Corsair: The Story of the Emden,* Hodder and Stoughton, London.
Low Head
Branagan, J.G. 1980, *George Town: History of the Town and District,* Regal Publications, Launceston.
Gott, K.D. 1984, *The Manned Tasmanian Lighthouses: Deal Island, Low Head, Cape Bruny, Maatsuyker Island, Swan Island, Eddystone Point,* St Kilda, Victoria.
Stanley, Kathleen M. 1991, *Guiding Lights: Tasmania's Lighthouses and Lighthousemen,* St David's Park Publishing, Hobart.
Wilderness in the city
Jerry de Gryse Pty Ltd 1996, *Cataract Gorge,* Jerry de Gryse Pty Ltd, Hobart.
Deeth, Jane, 1991, *The Gorge Report,* Launceston City Council.
The Pirate Pickwick
Ferguson, John Alexander, *The Tasmanian 'Pickwick Papers': Studies in Australian Bibliography,* Royal Australian Historical Society Journal.
Craig, Clifford 1973, *The Van Diemen's Land Edition of the Pickwick Papers: A General and Bibliographical Study with Some Notes on Henry Dowling,* Cat & Fiddle Press, Hobart.
Matthew Brady
Von Stieglitz, K.R. 1965, *Matthew Brady: Van Diemen's Land Bushranger,* Fullers Bookshop, Hobart.
Nixon, Allan M. 1991, *Stand & Deliver! 100 Australian Bushrangers 1789-1901,* Lothian, Port Melbourne.
The Chinese in Tasmania
Vivian, Helen 1985, *Tasmania's Chinese Heritage: An Historical Record of Chinese Sites in North East Tasmania,* Australian Heritage Commission/Queen Victoria Museum and Art Gallery, Launceston.
Eddystone Point
Stanley, Kathleen M. 1991, *Guiding Lights: Tasmania's Lighthouses and Lighthousemen,* St David's

Park Publishing, Hobart.
The storm of the centuries
Bureau of Meteorology 1975, *Storm of 22 March, 1974: Portland–Fingal Municipalities,* Tasmania, AGPS, Canberra.
The coroner who came to a sticky end
The Lisdillon Salt Works—A History and Site Guide, Department of Environment and Land Management, Tasmania.
Three naked outlaws
Lempriere, Thomas James 1839, *The Penal Settlements of Early Van Diemen's Land,* Facsimile edition, Royal Society of Tasmania, Launceston.
Ring, Maree 1993, *Martin Cash: Life after Bushranging,* M. Ring, Hobart.
Cash, Martin 1870, *Martin Cash: The Bushranger of Van Diemen's Land in 1843–4: A Personal Narrative of his Exploits in the Bush and his Experiences at Port Arthur and Norfolk Island,* J. Walch & Sons, Hobart.
Formula One on wooden bridges!
Green, Barry 2000, *Longford: Fast Track Back,* CopyRight Publishing Company, Brisbane.
Planned down under
Ewington, D.L., Clarke, M.J. and Banks, M.R. 1989, *A Late Permian Fossil Horseshoe Crab* (Palaeoimulus: Xiphosura) *from Poatina, Great Western Tiers, Tasmania, Papers and Proceedings of the Royal Society of Tasmania,* Volume 123.
Lupton, Roger 1999, *Tasmania's Hydro Power,* Focus Publishing, Edgecliff, NSW.
Ghoulies and ghosties and long-leggity beasties...and bunyips
Taylor, Harvey 1994, *The Tasmanian Bunyip: Alive and Well?,* Huonville.
Steppes and stones
Weeding, John Seymour 1981, *A History of Bothwell, Tasmania.* Drinkwater Publishing, Hobart.
Our pioneer radio-astronomer
Asimov, Isaac 1975, *Asimov's Biographical Encyclopedia of Science and Technology,* Pan, London.
Reber, Grote 1977, *Endless, Boundless, Stable Universe,* University of Tasmania, Hobart.
The honourable escapee
Mitchel, John 1988, *The Gardens of Hell: John Mitchel in Van Diemen's Land,* Kangaroo Press, Kenthurst, NSW.
Horton College
Pretyman, E.R. 1958, *Some Notes on Horton College, Once, a Well-known School near Ross, Tasmania,* Royal Society of Tasmania Papers and Proceedings, Vol 2 (1958).
'Eagle Nesting at Horton College', *The Mercury,* 28.10.1889
The man who shrank the world
Post, Wiley and Gatty, Harold 1932, *Around the World in Eight Days—The Flight of the Winnie Mae,* Hamilton,

London.

Gatty, Harold 1943, *The Raft Book*, George Grady Press, New York. (Available for viewing in the Tasmaniana Library.)

Gatty, Harold 1958, *Nature is your Guide: How to Find Your Way on Land and Sea by Observing Nature*, Collins, London.

Hospital in the bush

Box, Joy 1992, *111th Australian General Hospital, Campbelltown, Tasmania: 50th Anniversary, 1942–1992*.

Radioactive Rossarden

Hughes, T.D. 1961, *Uranium in Tasmania*, Unpublished report, Department of Mines, Tasmania.

Deddington Chapel

McPhee, John 1980, *The Art of John Glover*, MacMillan, Melbourne.

McCulloch, Alan M. 1968, *Encyclopaedia of Australian Art*, Hutchinson of Australia, Richmond.

Man's best friend…and worst enemy

King, Hilary (Ed.) 1987, *Epidemiology in Tasmania*, Brolga Press, Canberra.

Things that can hurt you

Sutherland, Dr Struan 1992, *Take Care! Poisonous Australian Animals*, Hyland House, Sydney.

Keyt, Terry 1998, *Dangerous Australian Marine Animals*, Macmillan, South Melbourne.

Tasmanian tiger—is it or isn't it?

Guiler, Eric R. 1985, *Thylacine: The Tragedy of the Tasmanian Tiger*, Oxford University Press, Melbourne.

Paddle, Robert N. 2000, *The Last Tasmanian Tiger: The History and Extinction of the Thylacine*, Cambridge, Cambridge University Press.

Two heads…

King, Hilary (Ed.) 1987, *Epidemiology in Tasmania*, Brolga Press, Canberra.

Index